HOW SYSTEMS FAIL

Your guide to building systems that last

HOW SYSTEMS FAIL

Your guide to building systems that last

SANDEEP BABBAR

Dedication

To all the incredible people I've worked with, thank you!

Your epic experiences and challenges have inspired this book.

Together, we've turned setbacks into opportunities and made messing up a fun learning adventure.

I appreciate all the lessons learned along the way!

Preface

Hello, curious readers,

Welcome to your backstage pass to the hilarious and baffling world of system failures. Have you ever wondered why smart systems do silly things or why good ideas fail spectacularly? You're in the right place.

Think of this book as a guided tour through the chaos of system disasters. Every wrong turn and malfunction leads to a story worth telling. We're not just talking about occasional glitches or hiccups. We're diving into the major blunders where companies pour millions (or even billions) into systems that spectacularly fail. It's like watching a high-stakes magic show where every trick hilariously backfires—educational, fascinating, and often downright hilarious.

Imagine a Rube Goldberg machine—those elaborate and overly complex contraptions designed to perform a simple task through a series of unnecessarily complicated steps. Each part of the machine interacts with another in a chain reaction, where a marble might roll down a track, hit a lever, which then releases a balloon, and so on, until finally, after a dozen steps, a light switch is flipped. It's ingenious yet inefficient, showcasing complexity for its own sake. That's how some systems operate—over-engineered and bewilderingly intricate.

We'll explore how these elaborate messes occur, showing how a single human error can turn a groundbreaking innovation into an expensive, useless apparatus. We'll also explore the human side of these technical disasters, like the time a well-intentioned update caused a major system crash. Often, it's the well-intentioned attempts to add 'just one more feature' that lead to overwhelming complexity. The drive to innovate can sometimes cloud judgment, resulting in systems that are more of a hindrance than a help. Through real-world examples, we'll uncover the pitfalls of over-complication and the importance of maintaining clarity and simplicity in system design.

By dissecting these intricate failures, we aim to understand not just how things went wrong, but how they can be made right. We'll learn to appreciate the elegance of simplicity and the value of clear, effective communication in building systems that truly last.

But it's not all about pointing out the mess-ups. You'll also hear about epic comebacks, accidental discoveries, and unexpected successes. It's a bit like baking—sometimes the recipe goes wrong, but you still end up with tasty cookies.

So buckle up for a tour of system screw-ups. We'll uncover why they happen, what we can learn, and how to dodge these pitfalls in the future. Whether you're a tech whiz, an eager learner, or just here for a laugh at these tech tragedies, there's something in this book for you.

Remember, failures are just as valuable as successes. They teach us important lessons and sometimes even show us better ways to win. So grab a cup of tea, settle in, and let's dive into this fun and enlightening journey together.

Contents

Introduction

Ever feel like the world is playing a cosmic joke on us?

Our world is full of systems often broken or slowly worsening, leading to many contradictions in our everyday lives.

For example:

- Poor countries that can't feed their people are busy exporting food to buy weapons and fight wars that make them poorer.
- Wealthy nations still can't balance their chequebooks, and often, they dive into recessions.
- Superpowers are fighting tiny nations and not winning.
- Revolutions fighting tyranny become the new bullies on the block.
- Celebrities get more famous for being famous – it's like a popularity loop on repeat.
- Countries championing the environment while funding polluters.
- Industries that generate vast amounts of waste advocate for sustainability, yet minimal changes are made to their production processes.
- Wealthy individuals donate large sums to charity for tax benefits while paying minimal wages to their employees.
- Nations declare wars on drugs while pharmaceutical corporations legally produce and distribute addictive substances.
- Banks offer financial literacy courses but profit from customers who mishandle debt and overdraft fees.

- Tech companies promote digital privacy while collecting and monetising vast amounts of personal data from users.

- Governments fund anti-smoking campaigns yet depend on to-bacco tax revenues to fill budget gaps.

- Clothing brands advocate for ethical fashion yet exploit labor in developing countries to keep costs low.

- Social media platforms claim to connect people yet often foster isolation and mental health issues.

Some folks blame it on "the system" and think we can fix everything with a new system.

Our world is full of these systems, many of which are in managed decline. Whether run by governments or big enterprises, these systems often limp along, patched up and held together by band-aid solutions. They promise progress and innovation, yet frequently deliver inefficiency and frustration.

The grand irony is that those in charge are usually too entrenched in their ways to see the need for real change. Instead of evolving, these systems muddle through, creating a landscape where contradictions thrive and true solutions seem just out of reach.

Imagine financial systems that topple over like a stack of dominoes, or educational systems that aim for innovation but produce uniformity. We're diving into the chaotic world of systems where anything that can go wrong, often does—spectacularly. From internet services that lag just as you hit the crucial moment of a movie to supply chains that falter over a single misplaced shipment, we'll uncover the often absurd and unexpectedly humorous ways systems fail.

This book takes a different approach. It says the problem isn't just one system or another; it's systems in general that are the trouble-makers. If we want to fix things, we need to understand how systems mess things up.

Building systems seems as natural to us as building nests is to birds, but taking a hard look at how they work? Not so much. When things go wrong, we'd rather blame something else than figure out what's really happening. It's like blaming your shoes for tripping instead of admitting you need to watch where you're going.

Understanding the intricate networks of systems that surround us is crucial because they form the backbone of our daily lives. From the transportation systems that move us, to the digital networks that connect us, and even the economic structures that sustain us—each is a complex system whose workings are seldom taught explicitly. Most educational curricula overlook the importance of 'systems thinking,' leaving many of us ill-prepared to navigate or manage the systems we depend on every day. By delving into how these systems function, and more importantly, how they fail, we can better anticipate challenges, devise effective solutions, and create more resilient structures for the future.

Technology systems are like a toddler with a new toy—full of potential and excitement but often messy and unpredictable. These systems are a fundamental part of our everyday lives, yet they are no strangers to failure. We've all faced the irritation of a self-checkout machine that just won't scan our items, or an app that decides to crash just when we need it most. From slow internet on a busy workday to smart home devices that seem to have a mind of their own, the mishaps of technology can range from mildly annoying to majorly disruptive. Understanding these systems better can help us minimise these frustrations and ensure that our digital tools are more reliable and effective.

The tech industry is particularly notorious for its systemic mishaps. Imagine the sector like a complex network of freeways where, despite the promise of speed and efficiency, frequent crashes and slowdowns are the norm. This represents a deep-rooted dysfunction in an industry that prides itself on pioneering innovation. Large organisations, which might appear sleek and efficient on the surface, often grapple with the same systemic issues that smaller entities face, particularly in managing technology systems. These challenges include poor communication, goals that don't align, and a stubborn resistance to change. For instance, consider a major initiative by a leading tech giant aimed at overhauling a government's technology infrastructure. Despite the resources thrown at it, the project was ultimately abandoned due to mismanagement, illustrating that bigger isn't always better; sometimes, it just magnifies the inefficiencies rather than rectifying them.

To paint a picture of how inefficient tech systems can be and the financial repercussions, let's delve into some compelling data. Every year, businesses globally lose an estimated $3 trillion due to failed technology systems, according to a report by the International Data Corporation (IDC). This staggering figure encompasses everything from complete system outages to minor glitches that cumulatively drain resources and productivity. In particular, the costs are not just the immediate expenses of fixing issues but also the lost opportunities and reputational damage that often follow. The inefficiency of these systems becomes more glaring when you consider that a significant portion of technology investments fails to meet their original objectives or deliver expected returns. This endemic inefficiency underscores the need for better system design, management, and foresight in the tech industry.

If technology systems were a builder, they'd be the one who promises a skyscraper but struggles to lay a solid foundation. Despite the flashy promises of streamlining operations and boosting efficiency, the tech industry often ends up costing businesses.

You might be wondering, "Did I really pick up a book that's all about how things fall to pieces?" Well, don't worry, there's more to it than meets the eye. This isn't just a showcase of failures; it's your personal guide to dodging system disasters. Think of it as the "What Not to Wear" for systems. I am not just pointing out the flaws—we're learning how to fix them and make everything run smoother. So, let's get ready to turn those system slip-ups into success stories!

So buckle up, grab your favourite stress-relief ball, and prepare to discover the wacky world of systemic failures. By the end, you might not be a certified systems engineer, but you'll definitely be a connoisseur of chaos, which, in today's world, is almost the same thing. And who knows?

You might even find the inspiration to create or tweak your own systems, because if there's one thing this book is good for, it's showing you the infinite number of ways you can mess things up. Let's learn how to mess things up a little less.

CHAPTER 01
ANCIENT LEGACIES

Roman chariots to space shuttles

Imagine technological progress as a driver in a high-performance sports car, eager to race ahead on a modern freeway. Instead of optimising his route with GPS and modern navigation tools, he insists on following a worn-out map drawn in the era of horse-drawn carriages. It's an absurd scenario, right? Yet, this is exactly what happens when our modern technologies are constrained by centuries-old decisions.

In this chapter, we'll explore how something as seemingly insignificant as the width of a horse's rear has had profound and far-reaching impacts on the technologies we use today. This isn't just about old standards; it's about the humorous, often baffling persistence of these standards through millennia. From the ruts in ancient Roman roads to the specifications of NASA's Space Shuttle, we'll see how historical choices continue to echo, influencing not just the paths we walk but even the heights we aspire to reach in space.

These historical decisions, made for reasons as mundane as accommodating two horses side by side, have unwittingly steered the course of technological advancements in ways that the original decision-makers could never have imagined. As we dive into these stories, we'll uncover a mix of unintended consequences and quirky legacies that highlight just how interconnected our past and present really are. It's a journey that's as informative as it is amusing, revealing the unexpected ways that history clings to us, like lint on a well-worn tunic.

Believe it or not, today's crammed peak-hour train from Central Sydney to Chatswood is riding on ancient Roman decisions. It wasn't emperors or generals, but the humble widths of chariot ruts—crafted for optimum speed and stability—that unwittingly set the standard for our modern subway cars. Fast forward a few millennia, and here we are, cheek by jowl, still feeling the ripple effects of those Roman charioteers who probably never imagined their wheel tracks would dictate how tightly you'd be squeezed between commuters today.

It turns out that the standard gauge for U.S. railroads—a precise 4 feet, 8.5 inches between the rails—can trace its roots back to these ancient pathways. The width was originally determined by the space needed to accommodate two war horses side by side in front of a chariot. This measurement proved so effective for the Romans that it became a standardised dimension, deeply ingrained in the construction of roads across their empire. These roads were engineered to last, and last they did, becoming the templates for the first railroads constructed during the Industrial Revolution.

As British engineers laid down the tracks for the early American railroads, they brought with them the familiar measurements of their country's tramways, which were themselves directly influenced by the ancient Roman standards. Ironically, this ancient standard was adopted not because it was deemed superior with any modern analysis but because it was deeply embedded in the infrastructure that preceded it. This adoption illustrates a perfect example of "if it isn't broken, don't fix it" thinking that overlooks potential improvements in favour of tradition.

The enduring legacy of Roman road engineering not only shaped the physical landscape but also dictated the flow of industrial progress well into the modern era. The width between the tracks determined everything from the size of train cars to the structure of tunnels and bridges, ultimately influencing how goods and people move across continents today. It's a classic case of historical decisions chaining us to a path that, while functional, was chosen for us by the needs and limitations of a bygone era.

As we stand (or more accurately, sit squeezed) in our subway cars, it's amusing yet somewhat astounding to realise that the design decisions made by Roman charioteers continue to affect how we design major transport systems. Their choices echo through time, a reminder that sometimes the tracks laid down by history are as literal as they are metaphorical.

As we chugged along from the age of steam engines into the era of space exploration, you'd think we'd leave old standards in the dust—literally. But no, the same measurements that snugly fit two horses' behinds side by side back in Roman times wound up guiding some of the most advanced engineering feats of the modern era.

Here's where the irony thickens: when NASA was designing the solid rocket boosters for the Space Shuttle, they weren't just thinking about thrust and fuel efficiency. They also had to consider an ancient standard because these boosters had to travel by train from their manufacturing site in Utah to the launch site in Florida. Yes, the fate of these cutting-edge technological marvels was tied to a railroad gauge established thousands of years ago for a pair of horse buttocks.

The journey of the boosters is a story of logistical acrobatics. To fit through tunnels and over bridges designed to accommodate the standard gauge, the boosters' size was strictly limited. This wasn't just a minor inconvenience. It was a critical constraint that directly influenced the final design and capabilities of what could have been even mightier marvels of modern engineering. Imagine telling the brilliant minds at NASA that their design parameters are based partly on ancient horse anatomy.

This quirky twist in the narrative of technological evolution shows just how deeply entrenched these old standards are in our systems. It's not only a humorous anecdote but also a profound illustration of how past decisions continue to shape our future—not just metaphorically but in the literal constraints they impose on our most ambitious projects.

As we aim to explore other planets and return to the moon, there's a surprising hurdle holding us back. Believe it or not, the standards for building some of our spacecraft are based on the space needed for two horses to stand side by side. This old measurement from Roman times affects how big we can make parts of our rockets.

Because the rocket parts had to fit on trains that use those old standards, they couldn't be made as big as we might have needed them to be. It's kind of shocking to think that our plans to explore space are limited by how wide two horses are.

This isn't just a funny coincidence—it's a real problem. If we want to go further into space, to other planets or the moon again, we need to stop letting old rules set so long ago hold us back. We need to create new standards that fit our dreams of space travel, not the width of a horse.

Old standards are like mullet haircuts—they keep coming back, whether we like it or not. While a retro hairstyle might be fun, these old rules aren't as charming when they pop up again. In critical areas like aerospace and telecommunications, they can really stir up trouble.

It's the same story in telecommunications. Many of the systems that handle our internet and phone calls are based on standards that were set decades ago. These old methods are often not suited for the huge amounts of data we send and receive today, leading to slower service and more dropped calls than we should have to deal with.

So, why do these outdated standards stick around? It's a lot like trying to teach an old dog new tricks—except the dog is a huge industry that's slow to change and set in its ways. Upgrading these systems can be expensive and complicated, so companies often stick with the old ways, even if they're not the best anymore.

Confronting the old guard isn't just a technical challenge; it's like trying to convince your grandfather to switch from his ancient flip phone to a smartphone. It's not just about the device; it's about changing a whole mindset that's set in its ways. Across industries, from aerospace to telecommunications, we're wrestling with legacy systems that are as stubborn as a mule and often just as outdated.

We've seen how a simple measurement intended for war chariots has dictated the parameters of our most advanced spacecraft and how old habits, once useful, can become barriers to progress.

This isn't just about rail gauges or rocket sizes; it's about a broader tendency in human systems to stick with the "known" long past its utility. It's about our collective reluctance to abandon the comfortable path, even when it leads us in less than optimal directions.

The reality is that every system, every standard, and every rule we follow today carries its own historical baggage, some of which may no longer serve us well.

We need to recognise when devotion to legacy systems turns from a virtue of stability to a vice of stagnation. In this era of rapid technological change, we cannot afford to be held back by outdated principles that no longer match the pace and needs of contemporary society. It's time for a critical reassessment of what we accept as "the way things are done."

As we've traveled from ancient Roman roads to modern space missions, it's clear that many of today's standards were set in a different world for different needs. This isn't just true for big things like railroads and rockets; it also applies to the little things we use every day.

Take the QWERTY keyboard, for instance. It was designed in the 19th century to slow down typing and prevent typewriter jams. Yet, here we are in the digital age, still using a layout meant to keep us from going too fast.

Then there's the placement of electrical outlets. These were standardised decades ago when homes had just a few electrical devices. Now, with our houses filled with gadgets, finding an outlet often feels like playing hide-and-seek. They're never where you need them, and there are never enough. It's like trying to charge your phone in a room designed by someone who thought the future would stop at the electric toaster.

These frustrating examples show how old standards stick around, even when they no longer make sense. They remind us that innovation isn't just about inventing new things; it's also about updating the old stuff that's holding us back. So, next time you're fumbling for an outlet or wondering why your keyboard layout is so awkward, remember: it's a call to rethink and modernise.

Buttons: The unseen hand of tradition

Imagine you're standing in front of the mirror one morning, buttoning up your shirt, preparing for the day. If you're a man, the buttons are conveniently placed on the right. But if you're a woman, you'll find them on the left. Ever paused to wonder why? This seemingly mundane detail is actually a relic of history, a perfect illustration of how our daily routines are shaped by the invisible hand of tradition—a tradition that may not always align with efficiency or logic.

The origin of this button placement is more than just a trivial fact; it's a reflection of societal structures and class dynamics from centuries ago. In the days of yore, particularly during the Victorian era, clothing mirrored social hierarchies and roles. Most men, irrespective of class, dressed themselves. Being predominantly right-handed, it was simply more practical to have buttons on the right side.

Women's fashion, however, tells a different story—a tale intertwined with luxury and service. In the past, buttons on women's garments were primarily designed for the wealthy, who rarely dressed themselves. This task was often left to maids. These maids, also predominantly right-handed, found it easier to button a dress or blouse from the opposite side as they faced their lady. Thus, buttons on women's garments were placed on the left, making the process smoother for the person doing the buttoning, not necessarily the wearer. It's important to note that this design detail primarily impacted wealthy women, as the average woman, who dressed herself, had little influence over such fashion conventions.

Fast forward to today, this practice persists, largely unquestioned in the realm of fashion. The rationale behind the original design has lost its relevance, but the design itself remains. It's a classic case of "we've always done it this way" prevailing over practical reassessment. This scenario isn't unique to the fashion industry; it pervades many aspects of our lives and work, often in ways we don't realise.

This curious case of button placement is not just a quirk of fashion history; it has real-world implications for modern manufacturing processes. The decision to place buttons on different sides for men's and women's clothing creates an unnecessary complexity in production, leading to inefficiencies and increased costs.

Imagine a clothing factory where garments are produced on a massive scale. Each production line must be configured to handle the unique specifications of men's and women's shirts. This means separate setups, patterns, and processes for sewing buttons on the right side for men's shirts and the left side for women's. This distinction might seem minor, but it introduces significant logistical challenges. Factories must allocate different machinery and labor for each type of garment, leading to inefficiencies. Studies have shown that standardising certain aspects of production can reduce costs by up to 20%, highlighting the potential benefits of rethinking these outdated practices.

Moreover, the additional steps required to produce gender-specific button placements increase the likelihood of errors. Misaligned buttons or incorrect placements can result in defective products that need rework or, worse, can't be sold. This not only wastes materials but also time and labor, further driving up production costs.

By reassessing and updating these long-standing practices, the fashion industry can reduce waste, lower costs, and enhance overall productivity—one button at a time.

In the business world, many systems and processes are the corporate equivalents of misaligned buttons. They may have been established under conditions that no longer exist or for reasons no one remembers. Like the curious case of the button, companies often continue to use outdated practices simply because they've been ingrained into the culture and operations.

In the world of business, old systems and processes often hang around like mismatched buttons on a shirt—awkward, unnecessary, and often misplaced. As curious as it might seem, the reason many companies stick to these old ways isn't always clear; it's just the way it's always been done.

Take the infamous Y2K scare, for instance. The world was in a frenzy because computer systems were about to turn their digital calendars from 1999 to 1900, thanks to their two-digit year coding.

It was a bit like realising you've been buttoning your shirts wrong for decades and now they might unravel right when the clock strikes midnight at the year's biggest party. Over $100 billion was spent globally just adding two extra digits to dates. While disaster was mostly averted, the massive expenditure highlighted how costly it can be to fix these 'heritage stitches' in our technological fabric.

Then there's the tale of the U.S. Department of Defence and their ambitious ERP system overhaul with SAP. Envisioned in the 1990s to streamline logistics and financial management, this modernisation effort turned into a $1 billion saga of complexities and outdated practices, never quite fitting the needs it was supposed to. It was like trying to sew a modern zipper onto a medieval tunic. After nearly a decade of tangled efforts and a billion dollars down, the project was abandoned. It was a clear example of how stitching new ideas onto old fabrics without a proper pattern can lead to a fashion disaster.

And who could forget the launch of Healthcare.gov? It was meant to be a sleek, online marketplace for health insurance but ended up more like a button missing its corresponding hole. The site's launch was plagued by crashes and errors because its backend was running on systems older than the idea of online shopping. Millions of users experienced the digital equivalent of a button popping off at an inopportune moment. The aftermath required frantic, costly fixes and was a painful reminder that new initiatives need to be sewn with fresh thread, not patched onto outdated fabric.

These stories from the corporate world demonstrate that clinging to outdated systems can lead to inefficiencies and failures as spectacular as a wardrobe malfunction at a gala. The cost of maintaining these legacy systems often far exceeds the investment needed to update or replace them. Just as the button placement on shirts can be modernised to better suit current fashions, business systems too can be streamlined to eliminate unnecessary complexities and boost efficiency.

By regularly reassessing and updating these long-standing practices, companies can reduce waste, cut costs, and enhance productivity. It's time to unbutton those outdated methods and embrace sleeker, smarter solutions. The lesson is clear: don't let your business be stitched up by the old ways; regularly update your systems and processes to avoid the pitfalls of legacy inefficiencies and stay in step with technological advancements.

Holding onto outdated practices isn't just an inconvenience—it can be a serious drag on efficiency and even result in costly blunders.

The insights gleaned from examining the stubborn persistence of outdated button placements aren't just a curiosity of fashion history; they offer a valuable lesson for businesses and individuals alike. This lesson stresses the critical importance of regularly questioning and reassessing our established practices, whether they're deep-seated corporate norms, daily personal habits, or long-standing business processes.

Just because a method still functions doesn't mean its functioning optimally or couldn't benefit from modernisation. For instance, just as fashion evolved to question and adjust the practicality of garment designs, companies too must evolve by examining the systems and technologies they rely on. This isn't merely for efficiency's sake, but also to foster innovation and agility in an increasingly competitive world.

Embracing change means recognising that improvement is always possible and often necessary. The challenge is to be willing to cut loose the old threads of outdated practices that no longer serve us well. It's about being proactive rather than reactive, making deliberate improvements not because we have to—facing a crisis or a system failure—but because we see the value in staying current and ahead of potential issues.

Ultimately, the call to action is clear: Regularly untangle and reassess the practices we take for granted.

The tradition of button placement not only serves as an intriguing historical anecdote but also poses practical challenges in everyday life. The majority of the population, being right-handed, finds buttoning garments with buttons on the left more cumbersome and less intuitive. This inconvenience for most women highlights a broader issue: the persistence of a design that caters more to historical context than to user convenience.

Moreover, the distinct manufacturing processes required for producing garments with different button alignments introduce unnecessary complexity and technical debt in the apparel industry. Each production line must accommodate multiple designs, which not only complicates logistics and increases costs but also echoes the kind of inefficiencies that many businesses face when outdated practices are maintained without question.

This scenario urges both individuals and industries to reconsider and streamline outdated standards that no longer serve their original purpose, reducing technical debt and enhancing overall efficiency and usability.

So, what does the tale of the buttons teach us? It's a nudge to be more mindful of the "why" behind our actions and choices. It's a call to challenge the status quo, to not accept "that's just the way it is" as an answer. Just as a tailor might reposition a button to better serve the wearer today, leaders and businesses are called to reevaluate and, where necessary, redesign their practices to better fit the contemporary landscape.

In essence, each time we button a shirt, we're presented with a small, daily reminder of how history shapes our present. Perhaps, it's time we start repositioning our own buttons, one shirt at a time.

Deep insights:

1. **Flexibility Over Tradition**: Systems should be like clay, not concrete. They must be mouldable and adaptable, ready to change as new needs arise, rather than being stuck in outdated formats just because they're historically entrenched.

2. **Broaden Education**: Bridge the gap between old standards and new possibilities by educating creators and implementers about the historical context of the systems they use. This isn't just about knowing the past, but understanding how it shapes—and sometimes skews—current technologies.

3. **Advocate for Flexible Regulations**: Push for regulations that allow for innovation. It's like lobbying for speed limits that adapt to newer, safer car technologies rather than sticking to limits set for older, slower models.

4. **Foster Collaborative Standards Setting**: Encourage discussions and collaborations across industries and sectors when setting new standards. Think of it as a roundtable where everyone from tech gurus to everyday users contributes, ensuring the standards work for all.

5. **Question Inherited Constraints**: Always question whether inherited constraints are still valid. What made sense in the past may hinder progress today, so be ready to redefine these boundaries.

6. **Future-Proofing Through Modularity**: Design systems with modularity in mind. Modular systems can be updated piece by piece, avoiding the need for total overhauls when new technologies emerge.

7. **Technology-Agnostic Standards**: Develop standards that are technology-agnostic, allowing for easy adaptation as new technologies emerge and old ones fade.

8. **Historical Inertia in Design**: The chapter illustrates how historical inertia affects modern design and functionality, emphasising that

many of today's designs are legacies that no longer serve their original purpose but persist due to tradition. This insight encourages us to critically assess whether current designs efficiently meet modern needs or if they are merely artefacts of past conditions.

9. **Cost of Conformity in Production**: The insight on the impact of gender-differentiated button placement on manufacturing efficiency sheds light on how small, historical design decisions can lead to significant inefficiencies and increased costs in production processes. This example serves as a metaphor for broader systemic inefficiencies across industries, where the cost of maintaining outdated systems or standards can be substantial.

10. **Cultural Persistence vs. Practicality**: The chapter explores how cultural traditions can override practical and ergonomic considerations, leading to designs that are less intuitive or efficient. This insight encourages questioning other "standard" practices across various fields to see if they are similarly upheld by tradition rather than utility.

11. **Innovation through Historical Understanding**: Understanding the historical context behind current systems and practices can be a source of innovation. By uncovering the original reasons for a design, innovators can identify which aspects are no longer necessary and can be improved, leading to more refined and suitable modern solutions.

CHAPTER 02
PREDICTING THE UNPREDICTABLE

I n our quest to understand the world around us, we often encounter systems—vast, intricate networks that govern everything from nature to technology. At first glance, the workings of such systems may seem straightforward. However, delve a bit deeper, and you'll uncover a universe of complexity where things often don't go as planned. In fact, they sometimes go spectacularly wrong. This chapter explores the enigmatic behaviour of complex systems, shedding light on why they often fail in unexpected and counterintuitive ways, and how this phenomenon is intrinsically linked to the broader theme of system failure.

At the core of many systems is a straightforward intention: insecticides are meant to protect crops, dams are built to provide water and power, and economies are structured to improve national prosperity. Yet, the reality of these systems' outcomes can be vastly different from their intended purposes. For instance, insecticides designed to safeguard agriculture can lead to widespread ecological damage, affecting biodiversity and disrupting ecosystems far beyond their targeted areas.

These examples illustrate a fundamental truth about complex systems: their outcomes are often unpredictable and, at times, diametrically opposed to their original goals. This phenomenon isn't just a series of unfortunate events; it's indicative of the inherent unpredictability of complex systems.

In the 1950s, biologists studying animal behaviour in controlled experiments discovered something profound: no matter how meticulously they designed their studies, the animals would invariably behave in unpredicted ways. This led to the realisation that complex systems, whether biological or mechanical, possess inherent uncertainties—behaviours that defy even the most detailed predictions.

This "Generalised Uncertainty Principle" of systems suggests that the complexity inherent in interconnected systems leads to unpredictable behaviour. Engineers and mathematicians often face this reality head-on; despite their precise calculations and designs, once a system interacts with the real world, it begins to behave in unforeseen ways.

This principle is especially relevant in environments where systems are interconnected and influenced by a multitude of factors. Here are some day-to-day systems where these phenomena are noticeable:

1. **Traffic Flow**: Traffic systems are classic examples of complex, unpredictable systems. Despite sophisticated models predicting traffic flow, real-world conditions like accidents, road closures, or even unpredictable human behaviour can lead to unexpected traffic jams and congestion. This makes real-time traffic management challenging and often requires adaptive traffic control systems to manage the unpredictability.

2. **Weather Forecasting**: Meteorology involves predicting whether through models that consider a vast array of atmospheric variables. However, the chaotic nature of the atmosphere means that small changes in one part of the system can lead to large and unforeseen effects elsewhere, making precise weather forecasting beyond a few days highly uncertain.

3. **Stock Markets**: Financial markets are influenced by global events, economic reports, and trader psychology, among other factors. This complexity leads to market behaviours that can often seem irrational and are difficult to predict accurately, despite the use of advanced financial models.

4. **Ecosystem Management**: In ecology, managing natural habitats involves understanding complex interactions between species, climate, and human activity. Unintended consequences can arise from actions like introducing or removing a species, which may lead to unpredicted alterations in the ecosystem.

5. **Healthcare**: In medical treatment, patients may respond unpredictably to medications or interventions due to the complex nature of human biology and individual genetic differences. What works for one patient may not work for another, or might cause unexpected side effects.

These examples illustrate how complex systems in different domains can exhibit behaviour that defies simple predictions, underscoring the importance of flexibility and adaptability in system design and management. Understanding and managing these systems requires continuous monitoring, adjustments, and sometimes even a complete redesign to accommodate new information and outcomes.

Imagine an enterprise system as a corporate potluck dinner. Everyone agrees to bring dishes that complement each other perfectly. In theory, this should result in a harmonious meal. However, reality often plays out more humorously and chaotically—much like dealing with complex enterprise systems in business. What should be a smooth integration turns into a mishmash of clashing flavours and unexpected outcomes, highlighting the unpredictability of complex systems.

Boeing's 737 MAX aircraft faced catastrophic failures due to software issues with the Manoeuvring Characteristics Augmentation System (MCAS). The integration of this system into the aircraft's design, combined with insufficient pilot training and poor communication, led to two fatal crashes. It was as if Boeing added a secret ingredient to a recipe but forgot to tell the chefs, leading to disastrous results. This example underscores the critical need for thorough testing and transparent communication in complex systems.

When Airbus was assembling its A380 superjumbo jets, they encountered significant delays and cost overruns because different plants in Germany and France used incompatible wiring designs. This misalignment was due to the use of different CAD software versions.

In 2012, Knight Capital Group deployed new trading software that inadvertently triggered a series of erroneous stock trades, resulting in a loss of $440 million in just 45 minutes. This was caused by a software configuration issue where old, unused code was inadvertently reactivated. Imagine bringing an old, untested family recipe to a potluck and realising too late that it's no longer safe to eat. The financial chaos that ensued exemplifies how overlooked details in system upgrades can lead to massive, unforeseen consequences.

These examples illustrate how even the best-laid plans in enterprise systems can go disastrously wrong. The Generalised Uncertainty Principle reminds us that complexity often leads to unpredictable outcomes, whether it's in the deployment of a new software tool or the organisation of a simple potluck dinner. By acknowledging and planning for these uncertainties, companies can better navigate the chaotic but always interesting world of large-scale systems.

The concept of "Climax Design" refers to the largest and most complex systems humans can build—skyscrapers that alter local weather patterns, massive ships whose engines might fail simultaneously, or sprawling cities that grow beyond their planned capacities. These systems often fail in ways that are as spectacular as they are unexpected.

The failures of complex systems offer crucial lessons. First, they teach us about the limits of human foresight and planning. No matter how advanced our technologies or detailed our designs, the complexity of interacting components within a system can lead to outcomes that nobody anticipated.

Second, these failures prompt us to reconsider our approaches to designing and managing systems. They highlight the need for flexibility, resilience, and adaptability in our plans. Incorporating feedback mechanisms, for instance, can help adjust a system's operation in real-time, responding to unforeseen changes and conditions.

As we encounter and interact with complex systems, whether in architecture, technology, or ecology, we must recognise and respect their inherent unpredictability. Understanding that systems may not always behave as intended is crucial in developing more robust, adaptable, and resilient systems.

Moreover, this acknowledgment pushes us to innovate in our approaches to planning and problem-solving. By embracing the mysterious ways of systems, we can better prepare for the unexpected, ensuring that our endeavours in system design are not only ambitious but also aligned with the realities of a complex world.

Deep insights:

1. **Predictive Paradox**: Embrace the concept that the more we try to predict and control complex systems, the more we may inadvertently contribute to their unpredictability. This arises because our interventions can introduce new variables and dynamics into the system. Recognising this paradox can lead to more humble and cautious approaches in system management, where constant learning and adaptation become central strategies.

2. **Leverage Chaos Theory**: Delve deeper into chaos theory to enhance system design and management. Small inputs can lead to disproportionately large outcomes in complex systems (the butterfly effect), which means that seemingly trivial changes or errors can cascade into significant impacts. Designing with an awareness of these sensitive dependencies can help in crafting systems that minimise negative cascades while enhancing positive outcomes.

3. **Anomaly as Opportunity**: Instead of merely correcting anomalies as they arise, use them as opportunities for deeper insights into the system's workings. Anomalies can act as diagnostics that highlight underlying flaws or strengths, offering a roadmap for strategic improvements. This approach turns unexpected behaviours into a tool for innovation and refinement.

4. **The Illusion of Control**: Remember, steering complex systems can feel like piloting a kite in a tornado. Sometimes, success lies not in exerting control but in skillfully riding the winds of chaos.

5. **The Wisdom of Weak Links**: In a network, it's the weakest link that teaches the most about strength. Strengthen your system by focusing on these weak links, not by masking them but by understanding and redesigning them to withstand unforeseen stresses.

CHAPTER 03
PROMISES VS. PERFORMANCE

Imagine trying to drive through a dense fog, where you can barely see next few meters. You move cautiously, guessing your way forward. This situation is similar to working with modern systems that seem simple and efficient at first. However, just like moving through the fog, using these systems often turns out to be more confusing and difficult than expected.

Enter the concept of the **"Functionary's Falsity"** It's a quirky term for a common phenomenon: systems promising one experience and delivering another entirely. Think of it as ordering a gourmet meal and receiving a fast-food burger, or more poetically, expecting a Shakespearean sonnet and instead, finding a cheeky limerick in your hands. This mismatch between expectation and reality isn't just a minor hiccup; it's a fundamental feature of how complex systems often operate.

Why does this happen? Because systems are built by humans, and humans are infinitely complex creatures with limited foresight. We design with optimism, imagining the best outcomes, the smoothest operations. Yet, like a blindfolded Rubik's solver, we can't always foresee the twists and turns that will lead us astray. Each move we make, based on partial understanding, can send us spiralling further from our goal.

The "Functionary's Falsity" is not merely an academic concept; it's a daily reality in the business structures we navigate, the governmental bureaucracies we encounter, and even in the technological gadgets we use. Each system, with its intricate web of roles and rules, often ends up delivering surprises—some pleasant, many perplexing.

As we delve deeper into this exploration, we'll uncover just how these systems, meant to simplify life, end up complicating it, often leaving us puzzled and, at times, amused. So, buckle up—it's going to be an intriguing ride through the labyrinth of system design, where every turn could lead to unexpected revelations.

The "Functionary's Falsity" in large enterprises often manifests as discrepancies between the intended purpose of systems or policies and their actual outcomes. Here are some common examples:

1. Corporate Efficiency Programs

Intended Purpose: Streamline operations, reduce redundancy, and increase productivity.

Actual Outcome: Such programs often lead to an increase in bureaucracy. Employees might spend more time complying with new efficiency protocols and filling out paperwork to track supposed improvements than actually working efficiently. The layers of oversight added to ensure compliance can paradoxically slow down processes, making the system less agile.

2. Customer Relationship Management (CRM) Systems

Intended Purpose: Improve customer relations and streamline communication between clients and the company.

Actual Outcome: While CRMs are designed to enhance understanding and service, they can become cumbersome, requiring extensive data entry that takes up valuable time. This can lead to employees interacting more with the system than with the customer, potentially degrading the quality of service and customer satisfaction.

3. Performance Management Systems

Intended Purpose: Measure employee performance objectively to enhance productivity and reward top performers.

Actual Outcome: These systems can lead to a focus on meeting specific metrics at the expense of overall quality or innovation. Employees might "game" the system by focusing on activities that score points, while neglecting unmeasured aspects of their job that are nevertheless crucial. This can stifle creativity and encourage a box-checking culture.

4. Automated Hiring Systems

Intended Purpose: Streamline the hiring process by efficiently sorting through large volumes of applications to identify the most qualified candidates.

Actual Outcome: Over-reliance on keywords and specific criteria can lead to the exclusion of potentially excellent candidates who don't exactly match the algorithm's parameters. This can result in a workforce that lacks diversity in thought and background, which might stifle innovation and adaptability.

5. IT Security Protocols

Intended Purpose: Protect company data and prevent security breaches.

Actual Outcome: Extremely stringent security protocols can sometimes impede employee productivity, requiring multiple authentications and slowing down system performance. This may lead employees to seek workarounds that compromise security, ironically making the system more vulnerable than it was intended to be.

Each of these examples illustrates how the complexity of large systems and the unpredictability of human behaviour can lead to outcomes that diverge significantly from original intentions. Recognising these "Functionary's Falsities" is crucial for leaders who aim to refine system designs to better serve their intended purposes.

The Solo Programmer vs. The Corporate Software Team

Imagine Alison, a passionate coder who loves to tinker with software projects in her spare time. Alison decides to develop a personal finance app tailored to her needs. Working from her small home office, she oversees every aspect of the project: she designs the user interface, writes the backend code, and handles the database management. Each line of code reflects her personal touch, and she understands exactly how each part of the application interacts with the others. Alison's project is her brainchild, complete in its vision and execution by her alone. She knows every nook and cranny of her creation, experiencing both its strengths and its shortcomings firsthand.

Contrast this with her day job at a large tech corporation, where she is part of a vast software development team. Here, Alison's role is sharply defined. She might spend her entire day writing functions for data processing, isolated from the application's broader architecture.

Her tasks come down the pipeline, defined by team leads or project managers, and her output is integrated with hundreds of other pieces, most of which she'll never see in action during development.

The software product that eventually emerges is the result of many hands and minds, not one of which has a complete grasp of the whole. Each team member, like Alison, sees only a fragment of the final product, contributing to a section without a holistic understanding of the end-user experience.

In this scenario, Alison's private project is a stark contrast to her professional environment. At home, she enjoys the satisfaction of creating something from scratch, understanding each element's role in the bigger picture, and adjusting the workflow based on immediate feedback from the running application.

At work, however, she is a specialist, her skills honed to perfection in a narrow area but disconnected from the overall product vision. This corporate setting exemplifies a common theme in large-scale systems: as the complexity of projects increases, the necessity for specialisation and division of labour becomes unavoidable, yet it often dilutes the sense of ownership and holistic understanding that comes with smaller, personal projects.

This example underscores the broader implications of system design in various fields, revealing a universal trade-off between specialisation and holistic understanding. It prompts us to consider how systems can be designed to maintain efficiency without sacrificing the comprehensive insight that enhances innovation and personal satisfaction in work.

Captain Pinafore

Gilbert and Sullivan, known for their humorous and catchy operas, often poked fun at serious topics. One of their characters is a naval officer who, despite his impressive title, knows more about paperwork than actual sailing. This character, let's call him Captain Pinafore, spends his days buried in forms, reports, and endless meetings about fleet management. He's so caught up in the bureaucracy that he's almost forgotten what it feels like to be on a ship, facing the sea.

This funny setup by Gilbert and Sullivan shows what's called the "Functionary's Falsity." It's a simple but important idea: people in a system can get so wrapped up in their specific jobs that they lose sight of what they're really supposed to be doing.

Captain Pinafore, for instance, is supposed to lead and inspire his crew, make sure they are ready for the sea, and handle actual sailing tasks. Instead, he's turned into a paperwork expert, far removed from the real action of sailing and leading at sea.

This character might make us laugh, but he also makes us think about something more serious in our workplaces. How many of us get stuck doing tasks that, while they might seem necessary, don't really connect with the main goals of our jobs? From tech workers to office managers, many can end up focusing more on the red tape and less on the real work or service their job is about.

Gilbert and Sullivan use Captain Pinafore to highlight a common problem in organisations: jobs can become so specialised and focused on small details that employees might not see or understand the bigger picture anymore.

This lesson is important for anyone who designs or works in systems. It tells us that while it's good to specialise, it's also crucial to keep everyone connected to the main purpose of their work. This helps make sure that everyone's efforts are meaningful and that the whole system works better towards achieving its true goals.

Imagine Captain Pinafore has hung up his naval hat and stepped into the corporate world as a Chief Technology Officer (CTO) at a bustling tech company, TechSails Inc. His mission? To navigate the company through the stormy seas of digital transformation and technological innovation. But here's the catch: Captain Pinafore, much like his days on the ship, gets tangled in the administrative anchors rather than steering the tech helm.

It's Monday morning, and Captain Pinafore arrives at his office ready to tackle the high seas of information technology. However, before he can even open his first cybersecurity report, he's bombarded with a flurry of emails about updating the company's software licensing agreements. By the time he looks up, it's noon, and he's scheduled for back-to-back meetings.

The first meeting is about the budget for new laptops—should they go for the high-end model or stick with the standard? He spends an hour debating the merits of extra RAM with the finance team, a discussion that feels more like choosing the colour of the boat than planning its course. Next, he's dragged into a meeting about the company's cloud storage options. Instead of exploring innovative solutions, he's stuck in the doldrums, comparing different service level agreements and compliance.

By the end of the day, Captain Pinafore has dealt with everything from printer malfunctions in the marketing department to an impassioned debate about which coffee machine app has the best user interface. As he leaves the office, he realises he hasn't done a single thing that actually moves the company's technology strategy forward. He's been so busy with the minutiae that the bigger picture is sailing off into the sunset without him.

Captain Pinafore chuckles to himself as he locks his office door, thinking, "I might have swapped the sea for the server room, but it seems I'm more of a Paperwork Pirate than a Tech Captain. Maybe tomorrow, I'll finally get to steer the ship."

The Operational Fallacy Unpacked

The "Operational Fallacy" captures the divergence between a system's intended functionality and its actual performance, often resulting in a product or service that strays from its original quality. Let's explore this through a familiar corporate scenario—the creation and dissemination of a company report.

The Evolution of a Company Report

Direct from the Analyst: Imagine a financial analyst at a company who prepares a quarterly earnings report. When the analyst completes this report, it is detailed, nuanced, and rich with insights directly from the source—her own research and analysis. At this stage, the report is in its purest form, much like an apple picked straight from the tree.

The information is fresh, directly applicable, and extremely relevant to those who know how to interpret it.

Managerial Review: Next, the report moves up to a manager. The manager reviews this detailed report, but with a specific lens— what should be highlighted to senior management. The manager edits the content, perhaps simplifying some of the more complex data to ensure it is understandable at higher levels without the need for in-depth financial knowledge. This stage can be likened to the apple being sold at a local grocery store. It's still fresh, but it has been polished and perhaps slightly altered (e.g., sliced or packaged) to appeal to a broader audience.

Executive Summary for Leadership: By the time the report reaches the executive team, it has been condensed into an executive summary. This summary focuses only on high-level insights, key figures, and a summary of financial health, scrubbing out much of the underlying data and analysis that may be deemed too granular for top executives' review. Now, the report resembles the apple that has been processed for mass consumption—still recognisable, but far removed from its original form, lacking the depth and detail that might be necessary for certain decisions.

Company-Wide Email or Newsletter: Finally, the report is distilled into a few bullet points in a company-wide newsletter or email. The nuances are lost completely, and only the most essential or most impressive figures are shared. At this stage, the report is like an apple turned into a commercial juice—sweetened, flavoured, and far from its original state, designed to suit everyone's taste but without the complexity or the freshness of the original fruit.

Each step in this process adds layers of abstraction and simplification, which are necessary to cater to different audiences within the company. However, these modifications can dilute the essence and the detailed insights of the original report. The Operational Fallacy here lies in the belief that the report, as it travels through the organisational hierarchy, maintains its integrity and utility at each level, whereas in reality, it often becomes a shadow of its original self, stripped of the critical details that might influence informed decision-making.

Recognising the Operational Fallacy in scenarios like the dissemination of a company report helps underline the importance of creating communication systems that preserve the integrity of original data and insights. Solutions might include providing different versions of the report tailored to the needs of various departments, or better yet, offering training that enables wider access to and understanding of the full report for those who wish to dive deeper.

This understanding encourages not just awareness but strategic changes in how information is processed and shared within a company, ensuring that all levels of the organisation have access not only to the conclusions derived from data but also to the rich, detailed insights that informed those conclusions.

The landscapes of modern systems often present scenarios so ironic that they'd be humorous if they weren't so impactful. Let's explore some stark examples where the "Functionary's Falsity" and "Operational Fallacy" play out in real life, offering not just moments of reflection but also those 'aha' insights into systemic inefficiencies.

Corporate Training Programs

Consider a typical corporate leadership training program. It's designed with the noble intention of crafting charismatic, strategic leaders who can inspire teams and drive innovation. Yet, what often emerges from these cookie-cutter programs are managers who are exceptionally good at internal compliance and navigating the corporate hierarchy—important skills, no doubt, but not the same as leading with vision in dynamic market conditions. It's as if you attend culinary school hoping to become a master chef, only to excel in washing dishes and managing the pantry. Essential, yes, but hardly the intended outcome of culinary mastery.

The Boy Scouts

The Boy Scouts were founded with the ideal of teaching young people to thrive in and respect the outdoors. However, an increasing focus on safety protocols and liability concerns has shifted the emphasis. Today, troop leaders might spend more time ensuring every form is signed and every rule is meticulously followed than actually engaging scouts with nature. The original mission was to build resilience and resourcefulness through real-world challenges; now, it might feel like navigating a bureaucratic labyrinth is the challenge they're most equipped to conquer.

International Peacekeeping

International peacekeeping efforts are initiated to stabilise regions and create environments where civil societies can rebuild and flourish. However, these missions often require military intervention, sometimes even leading to conflict. Deploying armed forces in the name of peace can seem as paradoxical as a firefighter carrying a flamethrower. The troops are there to help, but their presence can escalate the very tensions they aim to soothe, occasionally burning bridges they mean to build.

These examples provide 'aha' moments by highlighting how systems, despite being designed with clear objectives, can often stray dramatically from their intended paths. They reveal an underlying paradox: in the pursuit of specific goals, systems may inadvertently cultivate outcomes that contradict their original purposes. This disconnect not only challenges the efficacy of such systems but also calls for a deeper, more nuanced understanding and approach to system design and implementation.

As we wrap up our exploration of the sometimes baffling, often humorous world of systems, a few crucial insights stand out. Systems, those grand designs meant to streamline complexity and enhance efficiency, frequently end up weaving their own complex web, leading to outcomes that can baffle even their creators. It's a bit like setting out to bake a gourmet cake and somehow ending up with a pancake—still edible, but hardly what the recipe promised.

This journey through systemic misadventures—from overly rigid corporate training programs to international peacekeeping paradoxes—reveals a landscape riddled with the ironic twists of the "Functionary's Falsity" and the "Operational Fallacy." These aren't just catchy terms to add to our systemic vocabulary; they're crucial concepts that highlight the gap between intention and outcome, reminding us that the path from A to B isn't always a straight line. Sometimes, it's more like a squiggle drawn by a toddler.

Look critically at the systems you participate in or depend upon. Are they serving their purpose? Where do they deviate? How can they be improved?

The call to action here is clear: engage with systems thoughtfully. Challenge them, question them, and when necessary, redesign them. After all, if we continue to operate within systems without understanding their deeper mechanics—or misadventures—we're like sailors navigating without a compass, surprised to find ourselves lost at sea.

By equipping ourselves with a deeper understanding of how systems work—and sometimes don't—we become better prepared to navigate and improve the frameworks that shape our lives. Let's not just live in our systems; let's understand them, improve them, and sometimes, when necessary, laugh at their quirks.

Deep insights:

1. **Systems as Living Entities**: View systems not as static entities but as living, evolving organisms that require adjustment, much like a garden that needs tending based on the changing seasons. This perspective encourages continuous evaluation and tweaking of systems to better serve their intended functions over time.

2. **Hidden Costs of Over-Engineering**: Overly complex systems often suffer from reduced efficiency and increased costs, similar to a machine that's so intricately designed it requires constant maintenance. This insight advocates for simplicity in design to enhance reliability and user-friendliness, ensuring systems are not only effective but also sustainable.

3. **Legacy Systems as Learning Opportunities**: Instead of merely discarding old systems, view them as case studies or learning opportunities. Analysing why certain systems degrade or fail to deliver on their promises can provide invaluable insights into designing more robust and adaptable new systems.

4. **The Optimism Bias in System Design**: The chapter touches on how systems are designed with an optimistic outlook, often overlooking potential pitfalls. This optimism bias can be seen as a kind of systemic hubris—where designers and stakeholders predict the best-case scenarios while underestimating the complexity and potential for error. This mirrors a psychological pattern where people overestimate their control over events, a phenomenon that can lead to significant gaps between expected and actual performance in systems.

5. **The Cultural Influence on System Failure**: Systems do not exist in a vacuum; they are deeply influenced by the cultures in which they are created and operated. For example, a culture that values speed over accuracy might develop systems that prioritise rapid output over thoroughness, leading to errors and inefficiencies that were not accounted for during the design phase. This

cultural influence is often an unspoken yet powerful force that shapes the outcome and effectiveness of systems, contributing to the "Functionary's Falsity."

6. **The Paradox of Choice in System Complexity**: The chapter describes how systems intended to simplify life end up complicating it. This can be linked to the paradox of choice—the more options and functionalities a system offers, the more overwhelming it can become for the user. This paradox can cause decision fatigue, where the abundance of choices leads to poorer quality decisions or a complete avoidance of decision-making, which in turn decreases system usability and satisfaction.

7. **Metamodernistic Approach to Systems**: In response to the "Functionary's Falsity", a metamodernistic approach to systems might be proposed. Metamodernism navigates between the poles of idealism and realism, acknowledging system limitations while aspiring to transcend them. By embracing both skepticism and sincerity, system designers and users might find a more balanced approach, accepting imperfections in systems while still striving for improvement and innovation.

8. **The Quantum Uncertainty of Systems**: Drawing an analogy from quantum physics, one might consider the observer effect—where the act of observing or measuring something changes the object itself. In complex systems, the very act of trying to measure or optimise performance might alter the behaviour of the system or its users in unpredictable ways, thereby making the original measurements somewhat misleading or counterproductive.

CHAPTER 04
THE MIRAGE OF SUCCESS

Welcome to the backstage of the corporate magic show, where the tricks are not limited to pulling rabbits out of hats but extend to making entire problems disappear—at least on paper.

In this chapter, we pull back the curtain on the "Operational Fallacy," a pervasive illusion where systems, ranging from corporate bureaucracies to governmental agencies, consistently fail to perform as advertised, revealing a stark dissonance between what is reported and what actually is. This discrepancy not only misleads but often mismanages expectations at all levels, from the boardroom to the break room.

Imagine, if you will, a magician who convinces the audience that he can make an elephant vanish. The lights dazzle, the cloaks swirl, and sure enough, when the smoke clears, the elephant seems gone. Yet, behind the scenes, it's just cleverly concealed by mirrors and distractions. Much like in our corporate and public systems, the reality is there—massive and hard to manoeuvre—but cloaked in layers of reports, data, and bureaucratic tape that make it hard to see.

At the core of many systemic failures is a principle so pervasive, yet so often overlooked, that it has earned its own acronym: F.L.A.W., (Fundamental Law of Administrative Workings) which means "Things Are What They Are Reported to Be." This concept reflects the all-too-common practice within systems where the reality presented in reports, spreadsheets, and presentations becomes the accepted truth, regardless of the ground realities.

Let's consider an example from the corporate world, using Enron, a company that once dazzled shareholders with reports of profitability, groundbreaking innovation, and aggressive market expansion. Quarter after quarter, Enron's reports painted a picture of a corporate juggernaut. Executives boasted at conferences, employees believed in a secure future, and the media lauded their supposed success.

However, the reality was a far cry from these reports. Behind the façade of flashy PowerPoint slides and jargon-filled financial statements, Enron was hemorrhaging money due to mismanagement and poor strategic decisions, including the use of complex accounting loopholes and fraudulent reporting practices. The situation culminated in a spectacular crash when the company, which had been the darling of Wall Street, suddenly declared bankruptcy in December 2001, leaving everyone asking: "But the reports were so positive, what happened?"

This case exemplifies the F.L.A.W. in action. It reveals how systemic failures often stem from an over reliance on reported data, which, while neatly compiled and confidently presented, can mask underlying problems until they become too severe to ignore. This disconnect between reports and reality not only misleads stakeholders but can also lead to decisions that exacerbate hidden problems, setting the stage for eventual disaster. The lesson here is clear: systems must develop mechanisms to ensure that their reported realities reflect the actual state of affairs, thereby preventing the reports from becoming mere tools of illusion.

In modern systems, individuals often find themselves reduced to mere cogs in a machine, especially as the scale of the system expands. This section explores how the sheer size of a system impacts the individual's ability to influence or even interact meaningfully within it.

In colossal systems, such as government agencies or multinational corporations, individuals are often distilled down to numbers or data points. Their unique needs and circumstances become obscured by the volume of cases or transactions handled daily. This depersonalisation not only affects the quality of service or care provided but also diminishes the individual's engagement and satisfaction with the system. Conversely, in medium-sized systems—perhaps a regional hospital or a community bank—while there may still be a semblance of personal recognition, the growing pressures to 'scale up' can threaten this personal touch.

Imagine you're trying to order a custom cake for a special occasion. You call up a massive, automated bakery service renowned for its efficiency. You envision a cake that reflects personal tastes and aesthetics, something uniquely you. However, your call is answered by an automated system, offering you options A, B, or C from a preset menu. Want a vegan, gluten-free cake with a hand-painted design of your cat? The system responds: "Please select from chocolate, vanilla, or red velvet." Your personal preferences are swept aside by the bakery's streamlined, one-size-fits-all approach. This scenario, while simplified, mirrors the frustrations many experience when dealing with large, impersonal systems where the menu of options is vast but rigidly predefined, leaving little room for individual customisation.

This metaphor underscores a critical dilemma in system design: scalability often comes at the expense of individual specificity. As systems grow, the interface between the system and the individual becomes increasingly standardised to manage complexity, often ignoring the nuanced needs of its users. This not only leads to dissatisfaction but can also result in systemic inefficiencies where the 'standard' solutions offered are misaligned with the actual requirements of the individuals they serve.

The challenge, then, is to design systems that maintain their ability to cater to individual needs even as they expand. This involves innovating ways to incorporate flexibility within the systemic structure, ensuring that growth does not eclipse the human element so essential to the system's effectiveness and integrity.

In every large system, there exists a curious phenomenon where the quirks of human behaviour intermingle with systemic functions, often resulting in scenarios that are as absurd as they are instructive. This section delves into two such phenomena: Functionary's Pride and Hireling's Hypnosis, both of which highlight how individual perceptions can skew the operational realities of a system.

Functionary's Pride

This term describes a situation where individuals within a system, often those in middle management, overestimate their contribution to the organisations success. For instance, consider a middle manager who meticulously maintains a series of complex Excel spreadsheets. He believes that these spreadsheets are crucial to the company's profits, attributing every uptick in sales to his masterful data management. In reality, the spreadsheets are so convoluted that no one else in the company can use or even understand them, and their direct contribution to operational success is minimal. Yet, in the manager's view, these spreadsheets are the linchpin of the business.

At Kodak, a once-giant in the photography industry, certain executives played pivotal roles during the shift from film to digital photography. One particular manager was instrumental in developing digital camera technology. Despite his contributions to digital imaging, his insistence that digital cameras would not replace film led to strategic decisions that delayed Kodak's full entry into the digital market. He believed his understanding of film's superiority was a key asset to Kodak, even as the market rapidly shifted away from film. This misjudgment contributed significantly to Kodak's eventual downfall as they failed to adapt to digital trends quickly enough.

At Yahoo, a team of engineers believed their algorithm improvements to Yahoo's search engine were key to the company's success in the early 2000s. They focused heavily on tweaking search parameters and optimising ad placements, convinced these efforts were central to Yahoo's profitability. Despite their dedication, they failed to innovate at the pace of competitors like Google, whose algorithms not only delivered better search results but also integrated groundbreaking technologies such as machine learning. The Yahoo team's overconfidence in their existing technology prevented them from seeking necessary innovations, ultimately causing them to fall behind.

These examples demonstrate how the phenomenon of "Functionary's Pride" can manifest across different industries and lead to significant strategic missteps. In each case, individuals or groups within the companies overestimated their contributions or the effectiveness of their specific projects, leading to a lack of adaptability and eventual decline in the face of evolving markets. This misalignment between perceived and actual impact highlights the importance of critical self-assessment and adaptability within corporate structures.

Hireling's Hypnosis

This concept illustrates how routine and repetition can lead employees to follow nonsensical practices without questioning their efficacy. A humorous example of this can be seen in an office where, through a miscommunication, employees come to believe that wearing green on Wednesdays significantly boosts sales. This superstition becomes so ingrained that it turns into a ritualistic practice: the entire team dons green attire every Wednesday, convinced that their sartorial choices are driving the company's revenue, despite no evidence to support this belief.

Imagine an office where the coffee machine is believed to dispense not just coffee but luck. Every morning, employees form an orderly queue to perform a small dance before pressing the brew button, believing this ritual will increase their productivity and creativity for the day. As absurd as it sounds, this behaviour is reinforced by anec-dotal 'successes' shared among the staff, turning the coffee machine into a mystical totem of office lore. This scenario, while exaggerated, underscores a more profound truth about system behaviour: rituals and routines can often evolve into entrenched practices based solely on collective belief rather than any empirical effectiveness.

These example illustrate how systems can inadvertently encour-age behaviours that are detached from their intended functions. The quirks of system behaviour are not just a source of amusement; they offer valuable insights into how systems can be realigned with reali-ty. By understanding these behaviours, system designers and manag-ers can work to dismantle unhelpful myths and foster a culture that values critical thinking and genuine productivity over adherence to baseless rituals.

Systems can sometimes cultivate their own myths—delusions that persistently skew perception and decision-making. Two of the most pervasive of these myths are the Manager's Mirage and Orwell's Inversion, each illustrating how systems can distort reality to the det-riment of actual progress.

Manager's Mirage

This phenomenon occurs when leaders within a system believe that their activities, such as holding meetings, are inherently productive, regardless of the tangible outcomes. For example, consider a proj-ect manager who schedules back-to-back meetings to discuss project progress. In his view, each meeting brings the team closer to project completion because "things are being discussed." However, the real-ity is that these meetings consume valuable time without producing decisive action or results, effectively slowing down the project. The manager's mirage has him believe that motion equals progress, confusing activity with efficacy.

In the late 2000s, Nokia's management, confident in their market leadership, organised numerous meetings and committees to discuss the development of new technologies and strategies to compete with rising competitors like Apple and Android. The leaders held frequent strategy sessions, believing that these continuous discussions were crucial for keeping Nokia at the forefront of mobile technology innovation.

Despite the extensive meetings, the actual decision-making process was incredibly slow. These meetings often resulted in little actionable output and delayed responses to the fast-changing mobile market. The emphasis was more on process and less on outcome, leading to a situation where activity (in the form of meetings) was mistaken for real progress.

This managerial approach created a mirage where the executives felt they were making significant strides in adapting to new market realities, whereas in fact, they were merely spinning their wheels. Nokia's failure to decisively and quickly embrace a robust smartphone strategy, unlike its competitors who were rapidly innovating and capturing market share, led to the eventual decline of its mobile division. This inability to translate meetings into meaningful product innovations or strategic pivots is a classic case of "Manager's Mirage," where the perceived busyness of leadership was confused with effective leadership and market responsiveness.

This example serves as a cautionary tale about the dangers of equating activity with productivity, highlighting the importance of outcome-focused management practices in a rapidly evolving industry.

Orwell's Inversion

Named after George Orwell's keen insights into bureaucratic doublespeak, this concept refers to the confusing of inputs for outputs. In a typical scenario, a research team might spend extensive resources conducting studies and generating reports. The sheer volume of documentation is impressive, leading management to view it as an output—an end product—rather than as an input into the broader process of innovation. This inversion can lead organisations to celebrate the wrong milestones, such as praising the production of reports instead of the application of their findings to create real-world solutions.

Imagine a software development project at a large tech company, brilliantly structured and meticulously documented. Every procedure is followed to the letter. Weekly updates glow with positive metrics and milestone completions. Yet, when the launch date arrives, the software is riddled with bugs and lacks critical features promised to clients. The project was reported as a success because it adhered to all procedural protocols, yet it fundamentally failed to deliver its intended product. This story, while fictional, mirrors real scenarios where the process is celebrated despite the product being inadequate or incomplete.

These delusions are not just harmless misunderstandings; they can fundamentally alter the course of organisational strategies and employee actions. By recognising and addressing these distortions, organisations can better align their practices with their actual goals and avoid the pitfalls of celebrating form over substance. This section not only highlights the need for critical scrutiny within systems but also serves as a call to action for leaders to foster a culture that values outcomes over optics, ensuring that what is reported as success truly corresponds to real achievements.

In the intricate web of organisational structures, systems not only define processes but also profoundly shape the behaviours and expectations of those who operate within them. Over time, these systems cultivate what can be termed System-People—individuals who have not only adapted to but thrived under specific systemic conditions, often at the cost of broader efficiency or creativity.

System-People are typically well-versed in navigating complex bureaucracies and may even excel in environments that outsiders might find restrictive or dysfunctional. They have mastered the art of operating within the confines of the system, often developing skills more aligned with maintaining the status quo than pushing for innovative change.

Imagine Charlie, a mid-level manager in a large corporation, who has perfected the art of looking perpetually busy. To an onlooker, Charlie is always on the move, papers in hand, and engaged in serious conversations. He schedules back-to-back meetings, sends emails at all hours, and is constantly seen with a phone glued to his ear. However, beneath this flurry of activity, Charlie's actual productivity is minimal. His efforts, while visible, do little to advance real organisational goals but rather keep him in good standing within a system that equates visibility with value. This fictional yet relatable scenario underscores how systems can inadvertently incentivise appearances over substantive contributions, leading to a workforce more concerned with seeming busy than being effective.

This exploration into the realities inside systems has unveiled a world where appearances often eclipse substance, and operational fallacies can lead to significant systemic discrepancies. From the F.L.A.W. principle to the quirks of system behaviour, we've seen how systems can distort individual perceptions and actions.

Armed with this understanding, readers are encouraged to critically assess the systems they are part of. Challenge the norms, question the established truths, and advocate for a culture that values transparency and genuine productivity over mere activity. It is only through such critical engagement that systemic improvements can be made.

As we close this chapter, reflect on your own experiences: "What system illusions have you accepted as truth?" Consider how these perceptions have shaped your actions and think about steps you can take to foster a more reality-aligned approach in your professional and personal life.

By confronting these systemic puzzles, not only can we enhance our own effectiveness, but we can also contribute to creating more functional and transparent systems. This chapter serves as a roadmap for navigating the often convoluted realities of organisational life, empowering us to recognise, resist, and reform the systemic distortions that shape our world.

Deep insights:

1. **Transparency Mechanisms**: Systems should integrate continuous auditing mechanisms that not only check financial integrity but also operational efficacy to combat the Operational Fallacy.

2. **Reality-Based Training**: Incorporate scenarios that simulate the divergence between reported data and real-world outcomes in professional training programs to enhance critical thinking and problem-solving skills among employees.

3. **Systemic Feedback Loops**: Design feedback loops that actively involve insights from ground-level operations to executive decision-making, ensuring that top-level strategies are informed by on-the-ground realities.

4. **Escalation Triggers**: Implement data-driven triggers in systems that automatically flag discrepancies and anomalies, prompting immediate review and action to prevent escalation.

5. **Cultural Shifts in Reporting**: Foster an organisational culture where accuracy in reporting is valued over presenting an overly optimistic facade, reducing the chance of misleading stakeholders.

6. **Ethical Leadership Training**: Focus on developing leaders who prioritise ethical considerations in reporting and decision-making, embedding integrity into the core of organisational culture.

7. **Customer and Stakeholder Feedback**: Regularly engage with customers and external stakeholders to gain an external perspective on the organisations performance, balancing internal data with external perceptions.

8. **Reward Accuracy**: Adjust performance metrics to reward accuracy and thoroughness in data handling and reporting, not just outcomes based on potentially flawed data sets.

CHAPTER 05

INTEGRATED SYSTEMS, ISOLATED IMPACTS

ASWAN HIGH DAM

Back in the 1960s, Egypt was dreaming big, and not just regular big—pyramid big. It was an era of towering dreams and even taller engineering feats. Enter the Aswan High Dam, Egypt's bid to tame the Nile, the ribbon of water that had been Egypt's lifeline since the time of the Pharaohs. This was no small task; they were planning to put a leash on one of the world's most famous rivers!

The dam had a job description that would make any piece of infrastructure puff up with pride. First off, it was supposed to control the Nile's floods. These floods could either soak the soil just right for farming or party too hard and wash everything away. Next, the dam aimed to generate heaps of hydroelectric power. We're talking about enough electricity to light up homes, power factories, and maybe even toast a million pieces of bread every morning. Lastly, it promised to provide a steady supply of water for irrigation, turning dry dirt into lush fields year-round.

These weren't just random promises; they were solutions to Egypt's biggest headaches—like keeping the river from redecorating the landscape every year, making sure there was enough power for everyone, and growing crops even when Mother Nature was in a mood. The Aswan High Dam was going to be Egypt's superhero, wearing a cape made of concrete and generating enough electricity to make any villain think twice.

So, there they were, engineers and planners with rulers and blueprints, ready to give the Nile a makeover. They were about to embark on a monumental adventure to bend a river to their will and power into the future, all with a dam that was as ambitious as the pyramids themselves.

Once the Aswan High Dam was in place, acting all mighty, controlling the Nile turned out to be a bit more complicated than just flipping a switch. See, every year, the Nile liked to go on a spree, spreading nutrient-rich silt across the delta like a generous gardener. This silt was the secret spice that made the Nile Delta so fertile, basically the ancient version of a superfood for crops.

But with the dam blocking the way, the silt couldn't make its annual journey downriver. It was like the river's arteries got blocked—no more nutrients made it downstream. Suddenly, the lands that had relied on this natural fertiliser delivery service started to see their soil go on a diet of, well, nothing. The result? Farms started to struggle because, it turns out, plants are pretty fond of nutrients.

Meanwhile, another twist was brewing beneath the surface. The dam might have stopped the floods, but it also stopped washing away the old salts from the soil. Imagine throwing a party every year where the floors get a good scrubbing thanks to the hustle and bustle. Now, cancel the party, and all that dirt just piles up. That's what happened with the salts in the soil—no floods meant no natural cleaning, and the land started to collect salts like a hobby.

This buildup turned the once fertile fields a bit salty. The soil became so salty that even the plants that could handle a bit of sass from the soil started to throw in the towel. What was meant to be an agricultural boost from the dam turned into a bit of an agricultural bust, leaving farmers scratching their heads and wondering where all the good soil went.

So, between the missing silt and the salty soil saga, the grand plan of controlling the Nile had some pretty big wrinkles that no one really saw coming. The dam was supposed to be a hero for Egyptian agriculture, but instead, it ended up needing a bit of a hero itself to sort out the mess it made.

With the Aswan High Dam in place, Lake Nasser sort of became the Nile's new enormous backyard pool. But it wasn't just any pool; it was a giant bathtub where a whole new ecological party was about to start. With the river's flow under strict control, the lake invited some new residents—different fish species that thought Lake Nasser looked like a nice place to crash.

However, not all the native species were thrilled about these new neighbours. These newcomers started changing the local housing market, so to speak. They competed with the native fish for food and space, turning the original biodiversity into a bit of a battleground for survival. What was once a diverse and balanced ecosystem began to look more like a monopoly board where the new species were winning big time.

Downstream, the Mediterranean Sea was also feeling the effects of the dam, but it was a different kind of party foul. The silt that used to flow into the sea and feed the marine life was now stuck behind the dam. It was like the river had always sent a buffet downstream to the sea creatures, and suddenly, the buffet was canceled. The silt helped to build up deltas and beaches too, so with less of it coming in, the coastal landscapes weren't getting their usual makeovers.

For the local fishermen, this change was a big deal. Less silt meant fewer nutrients, which meant fewer fish hanging around. The fishing industry, which relied on these waters being rich with sea life, started to see their catches shrink. It was like showing up at your favourite fishing spot only to find out someone had put up a "Gone Fishing" sign on the fish themselves.

So, between Lake Nasser's new ecological mix-up and the Mediterranean's underfed marine life, the ripple effects of the Aswan High Dam were proving to be a bit more dramatic than just a controlled river. The whole system was connected, and changing one part of it was like playing a game of ecological dominoes—once you knock one over, the rest follow in surprising ways.

When the Aswan High Dam came into the picture, it wasn't just the river that had to adapt—entire communities along the Nile had to rewrite their way of life. For starters, the dam's construction meant relocating over 100,000 people from their ancestral homes in ancient Nubia. Imagine being told your neighbourhood was going to be submerged under a new lake, and you had to pack up not just your belongings but your entire life and move elsewhere. It was a massive upheaval that stirred a mix of loss, nostalgia, and the daunting task of building new communities from scratch.

Then there were the farmers, who for generations had danced to the rhythm of the Nile's floods. They knew exactly when to plant their seeds so that the floods would nourish their crops just right. But with the floods now a no-show, thanks to the dam, these farmers had to learn new steps. Traditional farming practices that had been honed over millennia had to be swapped out almost overnight for modern methods that many were neither familiar with nor fond of. This shift wasn't just about changing seeds or schedules; it was about changing a part of their cultural identity.

The broader social implications were just as profound. The Nile wasn't just a river in Egypt; it was a lifeline, a cultural icon, and an integral part of the Egyptian identity. Altering its flow on such a grand scale shifted its role in society. Festivals, songs, and stories that celebrated the life-giving floods of the Nile had to find new narratives. The relationship between people and the river changed, and with it, a piece of the nation's soul was quietly reshaped.

As communities grappled with these shifts, the social fabric of Egypt was stretched in new directions. Some threads strengthened as new opportunities arose from the changes, while others frayed under the strain of adaptation. The dam, intended as a beacon of progress, also cast long shadows over the social landscape, reminding everyone that when you alter a natural water course, the ripples touch not just the water and the land, but the hearts and lives of all who depend on it.

The saga of the Aswan High Dam serves as a profound classroom, teaching us about the Law of Unintended Consequences—the idea that actions, especially large-scale interventions, can have effects that are unanticipated or unintended. Despite its initial promise, the dam also scripted a series of environmental, social, and economic challenges that weren't part of the original plan.

One stark illustration of these unintended consequences was the emergence of fertiliser factories along the Nile. With the dam blocking the nutrient-rich silt from fertilising the delta, the soil became less fertile. To combat this, chemical fertilisers became necessary, and soon, factories sprang up to produce these fertilisers. Ironically, these factories began to consume much of the electricity generated by the dam itself. The hydroelectric power that was supposed to light up homes and power industries across Egypt was now being swallowed up to remedy a problem created by the dam in the first place. It was a cycle that no one had foreseen—using the dam's energy to fix the dam's own disruptions.

This situation underscores the critical need for holistic and adaptive planning in large-scale engineering projects. It shows that understanding the interconnectedness of environmental, social, and economic systems is crucial. Planners and engineers must think beyond the immediate technical challenges and consider the broader ecological and human landscapes that their projects will impact. They must anticipate changes not just in physical landscapes, but in the lives of people and the functioning of entire ecosystems.

Moreover, adaptive planning—being prepared to modify plans as new information becomes available and as situations evolve—is essential. The Aswan High Dam's story teaches us that large-scale systems are not just about building structures but about nurturing the environments and communities they affect. This means continuously monitoring impacts, listening to the communities involved, and being ready to make adjustments that minimise harm and maximise benefits.

The lessons from the Aswan High Dam are clear: when we pull a lever in one part of a system, the ripples can extend far beyond the initial splash. For future projects, whether they involve taming rivers or constructing new cities, the message is to plan with an eye on flexibility and a deep respect for the intricate tapestries of life that surround us. This approach isn't just about avoiding unintended consequences; it's about creating a legacy of sustainability and respect for the natural and human worlds we touch.

When the Aswan High Dam was envisioned, it was seen as a masterstroke of engineering, designed to harness a river that had flowed freely since the time of the pharaohs. Yet, its story teaches us that even the mightiest rivers and smartest humans can deliver unexpected lessons. This tale of the Nile isn't just about managing a river; it's about the humbling complexities of managing any large system.

First comes the need for systemic humility. The dam's narrative reminds us that we are participants in the systems we create, not their masters. Nature, with all its complexities and quirks, doesn't read our blueprints and rarely follows our scripts. It's like trying to direct a cat in a movie; expect it to do its own thing, often the opposite of what you need. In the world of system design, whether it's a software program, an urban infrastructure project, or an ecological intervention, humility is realising that we are still students of a classroom without walls.

Then there's foresight. This isn't just about looking forward; it's about looking wider. Foresight in system design means expecting the unexpected and planning for it. It's like packing an umbrella in the desert—not because you expect rain, but because you understand that the weather, like systems, changes. The Aswan High Dam planners might have benefited from imagining a wider range of scenarios, including those that seemed unlikely at the time.

Adaptation, the ability to pivot when reality starts straying from the plan, is crucial. The world around us is a moving picture, and our plans must be sketches, not static blueprints. Just as the dam required adjustments once its ecological impacts became clear, all systems need mechanisms for feedback and change. It's like having a good improvisation plan when your carefully planned event starts to go off-script—because, more often than not, it will.

The lessons from the Aswan High Dam aren't just about rivers or dams; they're about the need for a dynamic approach in all systems we engineer. Every system interacts with its environment in complex ways, often cascading into other systems and triggering effects we didn't foresee. Engineers, policymakers, and managers can look at the Aswan High Dam as a reminder of the need for systems thinking—a holistic approach that considers all potential interactions and respects the inherent unpredictability of complex systems.

Whether we're bending rivers, coding software, or crafting public policy, let's approach our creations with the humility of someone who knows they might get an unexpected reply. Let's design with the foresight of a chess player, anticipating several moves ahead, and adapt with the agility of a street performer, always ready to turn a stumble into part of the dance. Because in the end, managing systems effectively isn't just about the power to shape them—it's about the wisdom to let them teach us.

The Aswan High Dam, a marvel of human engineering, serves as a potent reminder of our entanglement with the systems we create and inhabit. It encapsulates a profound lesson in the dynamics of human ambition interfacing with the intricacies of natural systems. As we reflect on the dam's story, several key takeaways resonate, echoing through every venture that seeks to manipulate or harness nature's might.

The first lesson is respect for complexity. Complex systems, whether they are rivers, forests, markets, or cities, operate on principles that are not always visible or predictable. Much like a maestro conducts an orchestra without playing a single instrument, we must learn to guide these systems with a deep appreciation for their inherent complexities and hidden variables. The Nile, once believed to be a tameable entity, revealed itself to be a force that, although redirected, could not be wholly controlled or predicted.

Another insight is the necessity of understanding interactions within systems. Each intervention we make—whether building a dam or designing a cityscape—ripples across the network of interconnected elements. The dam's impact on soil fertility, water salinity, and local ecosystems provides a textbook case of how altering one component of a system can unleash a cascade of unintended consequences. Like dominos in slow motion, each change initiates another, often in ways we can scarcely anticipate.

Lastly, we come to the dance with nature. This relationship is perhaps the most delicate and crucial of all. While human ambition drives us to reach, build, and innovate, nature operates on a scale of complexity and time that dwarfs our own. Our efforts to lead this dance often see us stepping on nature's toes. The Aswan High Dam reminds us that while we can choreograph the steps, it is nature that provides the music and the rhythm. Our plans must move with the currents she creates, not against them.

DDT: From cure to curse

DDT, once celebrated as a groundbreaking chemical, epitomises the unintended consequences that can emerge from technological solutions. Initially developed to combat diseases and agricultural pests, DDT quickly became a staple in global efforts to improve public health and food security. Its potent insecticidal properties made it an invaluable tool in the mid-20th century, offering a glimpse into the potential of synthetic chemicals to harness nature for human benefit. However, this initial triumph soon revealed a darker side, as the pervasive use of DDT began to unveil its detrimental impact on the environment, transforming it from a miracle solution into a significant ecological menace.

The story of DDT serves as a profound lesson in the dynamics of systemic innovation and failure. It highlights a recurrent theme in the development and deployment of new technologies: while they may address specific issues effectively, they often trigger a cascade of unintended effects that can complicate or worsen other problems. This phenomenon underscores the essential complexity of systems—how they are interlinked and how changes in one area can reverberate unexpectedly across others. By examining the trajectory of DDT, from its zenith as a 'miracle chemical' to its nadir as an environmental pariah, we can better understand the inherent challenges of managing systems that are deeply intertwined with natural and human ecosystems. This exploration aligns seamlessly with the broader narrative of our book, emphasising that systems, no matter how well-intentioned, are susceptible to failures that can sometimes eclipse their intended benefits.

In 1939, a Swiss chemist named Paul Hermann Müller hit the jackpot in the world of science by discovering that DDT, a nifty little chemical, could kill bugs faster than a flyswatter on a hot day.

When World War II rolled around, DDT took center stage, keeping soldiers and civilians alike free from the itchy clutches of typhus and malaria. It was like a superhero cape for entire populations, swooping in to drop malaria rates and boost morale. Back at the farm, crops were thriving too, thanks to DDT keeping greedy pests at bay, which meant more food on the table during tough times. People were singing praises, and DDT quickly became the darling of the chemical world.

The cherry on top came in 1948 when Müller snagged a Nobel Prize for his bug-busting breakthrough. It wasn't just a pat on the back for being a bug killer, but a nod to the hope that diseases carrying misery across the globe could finally be beaten back. Winning the

Nobel Prize was like rolling out the red carpet for DDT, crowning it as a miracle worker in a world eager for easy solutions.

As DDT became a fixture in agricultural and public health programs worldwide, troubling signs began to surface about its broader ecological impact. Scientists noticed that DDT was not simply disappearing into the environment; it was persisting, entering waterways, and accumulating in the fatty tissues of animals. This phenomenon, known as biomagnification, became particularly evident in top predators such as birds of prey.

Reports began to emerge of thinning eggshells and declining populations among species like the bald eagle and peregrine falcon, signalling that DDT's environmental footprint was far more complex and destructive than previously understood. These early signs sparked a series of scientific inquiries into the broader ecological consequences of widespread DDT use.

Pioneering studies in the late 1950s and early 1960s began to draw direct correlations between DDT and ecological degradation. Researchers demonstrated how DDT accumulated in the food chain, reaching lethal concentrations in higher predators, which suffered from reproductive failures and population declines as a result. Aquatic ecosystems were particularly vulnerable, with DDT runoff from agricultural fields leading to declines in fish populations, which in turn affected the species that depended on them. These findings challenged the prevailing notion that DDT was a benign saviour of modern agriculture and public health, unveiling a troubling trade-off between its benefits and the long-term health of ecosystems.

The shift from scientific evidence to public awareness and policy change was significantly influenced by Rachel Carson, a marine biologist whose seminal work "Silent Spring" was published in 1962. Carson's book synthesised the scientific research on DDT and presented it to a lay audience in a compelling narrative that highlighted the chemical's insidious effects on nature and human health. "Silent Spring" did not just criticise DDT; it questioned the entire approach to pest control and the unchecked use of pesticides. Carson's powerful advocacy played a crucial role in catalysing environmental movements and provoked a reevaluation of pesticide regulations in the

United States and beyond. Her work stirred an ecological conscious-
ness among the public and lawmakers alike, leading to the eventual
banning of DDT in the United States in 1972 and sparking a global
conversation about sustainable pest management practices.

The growing body of scientific evidence and increased public
awareness, largely fuelled by Rachel Carson's advocacy, led to significant regulatory changes concerning DDT. In 1972, the United States
Environmental Protection Agency (EPA) issued a ban on DDT, citing
its adverse environmental effects, particularly on wildlife, as well as
potential risks to human health. This decision marked a pivotal shift
in environmental policy and was a critical moment in the broader
environmental movement. Following the U.S. ban, many other countries gradually phased out DDT or imposed strict regulations on its
use. These policy responses reflected a growing consensus about the
need for more stringent controls over pesticide use and a greater consideration for ecological impacts in regulatory practices.

The backlash against DDT and the recognition of its ecological
impacts catalysed a fundamental shift in how societies manage pests.
The crisis precipitated by DDT's ecological damages highlighted the
drawbacks of relying solely on chemical solutions to control pests.
In response, there was a significant move towards Integrated Pest
Management (IPM), an approach that emphasises the use of a variety
of pest control techniques. IPM strategies include biological control,
using natural predators or parasites of pests; cultural practices, such as
crop rotation and selecting disease-resistant crop varieties; mechanical
and physical controls, like trapping or creating barriers; and chemical
methods, applied in a targeted and judicious manner. This paradigm
shift not only aimed to reduce reliance on chemical pesticides but
also promoted more sustainable, environmentally friendly methods
that consider the entire ecosystem. The shift towards IPM represented a systemic change in agricultural practices, reflecting a deeper
understanding of the complex interactions within ecosystems and a
more nuanced approach to managing agricultural and public health
challenges.

The saga of DDT serves as a profound lesson in the importance
of considering the broader, systemic impacts of any new technology

or solution, particularly those intended to interact with the environment. The initial celebration of DDT's effectiveness overlooked its long-term ecological and health consequences. This oversight underscores a critical lesson: innovations must be evaluated not just for their immediate benefits but also for their potential to cause widespread and lasting effects. Systemic thinking demands a holistic approach, assessing how new interventions might ripple through environmental, social, and economic systems. The DDT experience illustrates the necessity of this comprehensive evaluation, as the failure to do so can lead to severe unintended consequences that may be irreversible and far-reaching.

DDT's history also highlights the need for adaptive management in regulatory and technological frameworks. Adaptive management is an iterative decision-making process that adjusts approaches based on the outcomes and new information. This kind of flexibility could have mitigated some of DDT's negative impacts if earlier signs of environmental damage had been acted upon swiftly. The concept advocates for systems to be designed with the capacity for modification as new data becomes available, ensuring that policies and technologies remain aligned with the best available science and societal values. Such adaptability is crucial in managing complex systems where initial conditions can rarely predict long-term outcomes accurately.

Finally, the DDT narrative powerfully demonstrates the role of advocacy and public awareness in driving systemic change. Rachel Carson's "Silent Spring" was instrumental in illuminating the dangers of DDT, sparking a major shift in public opinion and policy. This case exemplifies how informed advocacy can challenge and alter the trajectory of technological applications and regulatory landscapes. It shows that public and scientific advocacy are not just about raising awareness but are vital to activating the levers of policy change and ensuring that systemic adjustments reflect both scientific understanding and public values. The engagement of an informed public is often the critical force that compels industries and governments to consider more sustainable and responsible practices.

Together, these lessons from the DDT experience offer vital insights for managing complex systems and preventing future systemic failures. They underscore the need for holistic thinking, flexible regulatory environments, and active public engagement to navigate the intricate challenges posed by new technologies and their integration into our lives and environments.

This chapter urges professionals, policymakers, and the public to adopt a proactive and informed approach to system management. It's crucial to champion practices that prioritise long-term sustainability over short-term gains and to advocate for policies that require rigorous impact assessments before new technologies are widely implemented. By fostering a culture of responsible innovation, we can help ensure that future technological advances serve both our immediate needs and the health of our planet.

The tale of DDT goes beyond a historical account of a pesticide; it serves as a profound lesson in the complexities of system failures. It teaches us that failures often stem not from a lack of innovation but from a failure to understand the full scope of systemic interactions and long-term impacts. This story enriches the broader discussion on systemic failures by highlighting the importance of integrating scientific rigour, ethical considerations, and public engagement in the development and management of new technologies. As we move forward, let the DDT experience remind us of our responsibility to navigate the intricate web of systems with foresight and care, ensuring that our actions today do not become the systemic failures of tomorrow.

Deep insights:

1. **Systems Thinking in Design**: Understanding that every component in a system is connected is crucial. Changes to one part can have unexpected consequences on others. For instance, the Aswan Dam's impact on silt distribution demonstrates how alterations in one area (river flow) can adversely affect distant but connected systems (agricultural fertility, coastal marine life). This teaches us the importance of adopting a holistic approach in systems design, considering all potential ripple effects.

2. **Anticipating Unintended Consequences**: The story of the Aswan Dam serves as a stark reminder of the Law of Unintended Consequences. This insight presses the need for scenario planning and risk assessment in system design to foresee and mitigate potential negative outcomes. It suggests expanding the analytical horizon to include not just the most likely outcomes but also less probable scenarios that could have significant impacts.

3. **Respect for Complexity:** Every system has hidden depths; misunderstanding its complexity can lead to oversimplification that undermines the intended outcomes.

4. **Cultivate Systemic Humility:** Acknowledge the limits of control and understanding. Systems often behave in unexpected ways, despite the precision of our plans.

5. **Integrate, Don't Dictate:** Systems should whisper into the existing chorus of community and environment, not shout over it.

6. **Wisdom of Water:** Like water, a good system finds its strength not in resisting change but in its capacity to flow and adapt to the contours before it.

7. **Philosophy of Failures:** Every misstep in a system is a stepping stone to deeper understanding. Celebrate failures—they're the earnest tuition fees paid for wisdom.

8. **The Balloon Effect:** Just like blowing up a balloon, pumping more air (or growth) into a system will expand it until it potentially pops. When designing systems, it's crucial to install a 'pressure valve'—a way to let off steam when growth starts stretching the seams. This could mean having flexible policies that adapt to growth, or escape routes for when the system starts to overheat.

9. **The Elastic Band Principle:** Systems often behave like elastic bands. Stretch them too far with growth, and they might snap back painfully. The key is maintaining an elasticity that allows for expansion but also retracts smoothly to maintain control. It's about finding that sweet spot where growth doesn't lead to a painful snap.

10. **The Jenga Paradox:** Imagine building a tower of Jenga blocks, each block representing a new addition or change to the system. The taller it grows, the more precarious it becomes. Here's the twist: just like in Jenga, the challenge isn't just about growing taller but also knowing which blocks to pull out to keep the structure stable—highlighting the importance of strategic subtraction as much as addition.

11. **The Gardener's Strategy:** A gardener doesn't just plant seeds; they prune and weed, ensuring healthy growth without letting any one plant overshadow the others. Systems need similar gardening—pruning outdated parts and weeding out inefficiencies to allow healthy growth across all areas.

CHAPTER 06
BEYOND CONTROL

Systems, like dance partners, are dynamic and alive, responding to subtle cues and gentle guidance. They do not respond well to force; instead, they require understanding and finesse to navigate their rhythms and flows. Here, we will explore not just how to move, but how to anticipate and adapt, ensuring that every step you take within your organisation leads to progress and harmony.

The Puppet Master's Dilemma

Imagine being a puppeteer who is skilled at handling one or two puppets using a few strings. Each string's function is clear, the movements are manageable, and you can easily create the desired performance. But what if the number of puppets and strings increases significantly? The task becomes much more difficult. The strings may tangle, the puppets might collide, and the performance turns chaotic.

This is akin to what happened with Czar Alexander. His vast empire was like a complex set of puppets with countless strings. The more he tried to control every aspect—from political affairs and economic policies to social issues—the more he found himself caught in a web of administrative complexity. His story vividly illustrates the Fundamental Law of Administrative Workings (F.L.A.W.): as systems grow in complexity, controlling them effectively becomes increasingly challenging.

Czar Alexander's empire was vast and diverse, and his attempts to manage every aspect of it were akin to trying to juggle an ever-increasing number of balls. The more he juggled, the more likely he was to drop one. He faced the inherent challenge of overseeing an intricate administrative system where the connections between cause and effect were not always clear. His experience teaches us that in any complex system—whether a government, a corporation, or any large organisation—trying to maintain tight control over every detail can lead to unexpected difficulties and diminished effectiveness.

The Potemkin Village Effect: Beyond the Façade

Enter the Potemkin Village Effect (P.V.E.), named after the deceptive façades erected to impress Empress Catherine II. This metaphor extends to modern organisations that create impressive-looking systems achieving little. Like a stage set that looks like a bustling town from afar but is merely a series of facades, organisations often construct elaborate systems that fail to address underlying issues. By understanding this effect, we learn to look beyond the superficial to the structural, ensuring our systems are robust and effective, not just impressive at first glance.

In the modern corporate world, the Potemkin Village Effect can be seen in companies that focus heavily on their outward appearance—glossy marketing materials, state-of-the-art headquarters, and polished presentations—while ignoring the fundamental issues plaguing their operations. Such organisations may impress stakeholders in the short term but struggle with long-term sustainability and success. The key takeaway here is to build systems that are not only impressive on the surface but also effective and resilient underneath.

Volkswagen, one of the largest automobile manufacturers globally, prided itself on producing vehicles that met rigorous environmental standards. The company heavily marketed its diesel vehicles as being both fuel-efficient and compliant with the strictest emission regulations in the world.

Volkswagen's deployment of "defeat devices" in diesel engines is a textbook example of the Potemkin Village Effect. These devices were designed to activate emissions controls only during laboratory testing, making the cars appear to comply with environmental standards. However, once on the road, the vehicles emitted pollutants at levels up to 40 times higher than what was legally allowed.

The scandal came to light in 2015 when the Environmental Protection Agency (EPA) discovered the discrepancies in emissions during extended road tests. This revelation shocked the automotive world and the public, leading to a massive recall, numerous lawsuits, and significant financial penalties for VW. Moreover, it severely damaged Volkswagen's reputation, particularly regarding its commitment to environmental sustainability.

The Volkswagen case serves as a powerful lesson about the dangers of prioritising surface appearances over genuine adherence to ethical and regulatory standards. It emphasises the importance of aligning a company's outward portrayal with its actual practices to avoid long-term damage to trust and credibility. This example underscores the broader implications of the Potemkin Village Effect, where deceptive appearances can lead to significant consequences for stakeholders and the environment.

Catalytic Managership: Gardening Over Sculpting

Catalytic Managership is like being a gardener rather than a sculptor. Instead of aggressively moulding and pushing for change, this philosophy is about tending, pruning, and removing obstacles that hinder growth. Imagine a chemist using catalysts in a lab. A catalyst facilitates the process, making it easier and smoother without becoming part of the outcome. Similarly, catalytic leaders focus on enabling natural processes and removing barriers to organisational energy and creativity.

Consider Mahatma Gandhi, whose leadership catalysed India's push for independence. He didn't enforce change through force but empowered people, enabling a natural movement towards freedom. In the business world, leaders at companies like Google have implemented the "20% time" rule, encouraging employees to work on projects that interest them. This policy has led to significant innovations like Gmail and AdSense, showcasing how a catalytic approach can yield substantial breakthroughs.

Gandhi's approach to leadership was fundamentally different from traditional, top-down methods. He believed in the power of the people and focused on removing the obstacles that prevented them from achieving their potential. This approach can be incredibly effective in modern organisations, where fostering an environment that encourages creativity and innovation can lead to significant breakthroughs and improvements.

Designing Flexible Systems

When designing organisational systems, aim for flexibility that accommodates individual differences and adapts to changing circumstances. Imagine systems as articles of clothing: tight jeans represent rigid systems that look good but restrict movement, while sweatpants symbolise flexible systems offering comfort and adaptability. Similarly, organisational systems should avoid rigidity that stifles creativity and growth, ensuring longevity and continued relevance.

The most effective systems are those that do not go against the grain of natural human behaviours but rather enhance and facilitate them.

Consider the example of a playground slide: it's a simple yet perfect illustration of a system designed to work with gravity—a natural, unstoppable force. By positioning a slide to utilise downhill momentum, children can enjoy a fun and effortless ride without the need for additional energy or force. Similarly, when designing organisational systems, leaders should aim to harness the natural flows of work processes, employee behaviours, and market dynamics. For instance, instead of enforcing a rigid schedule that might clash with peak productivity times, a system that allows for flexible work hours could capitalise on when employees are most energetic and focused. By aligning system design with these natural tendencies, organisations can achieve smoother operations and enhance overall efficiency, effectively letting gravity do the work.

Breaking Down Power

Breaking down power means spreading it out so that no one place or person holds too much of it. This idea is like having a company or government where many different people make decisions, not just the ones at the top. This can make a company or government more flexible and better able to respond to new situations or problems.

For example, some companies, like Zappos, use a system called holacracy. In holacracy, teams organise themselves and make their own decisions instead of waiting for orders from above. This helps Zappos quickly adapt to new market trends and encourages a culture where everyone feels responsible and involved. Similarly, when governments spread power out more, they can be more in tune with what people need locally and respond more effectively.

Embracing Complexity: Lessons from Nature

Nature is a rich source of inspiration for managing complex systems effectively. It shows us how flexibility, adaptation, and decentralisation are key to thriving in a dynamic environment.

Ecosystems are complex networks involving diverse species and environmental factors. Each species plays a role that affects and is affected by others, creating a system that is robust and adaptable. For example, in a forest ecosystem, there are numerous plants, animals, and microbes interacting in ways that recycle nutrients, regulate population sizes, and maintain ecological balance. No single species controls the ecosystem; rather, it thrives by continually adapting to changes such as fires, storms, or droughts.

Ant colonies are another example of nature's decentralised systems. There is no central authority directing each ant's actions. Instead, ants communicate using pheromones to inform each other about food sources or threats. This allows them to make collective decisions efficiently and adapt quickly to new information, such as finding the shortest path to food or changing tasks based on the colony's needs.

Birds in flight, particularly those that flock like starlings, demonstrate complex, adaptive behaviour that is decentralised. Each bird in the flock responds to the movements of its neighbours, allowing the entire group to manoeuvre and change direction almost instantaneously. This capability enhances the flock's ability to evade predators, maintain course over long migrations, and manage the group's energy use.

Coral reefs are among the most diverse and complex ecosystems on Earth. They thrive through a decentralised network of organisms that depend on each other for survival. For example, coral polyps, algae, and various marine creatures form a symbiotic relationship; the algae provide the corals with nutrients through photosynthesis, while the corals provide the algae with a protected environment and the compounds they need to photosynthesise. This intricate balance allows coral reefs to adapt and thrive in nutrient-poor waters, showcasing how decentralised cooperation can lead to resilience and sustainability.

Underneath the forest floor, there exists a complex, hidden network of fungi called mycorrhizae, which connect the roots of different plants. This network, often referred to as the "Wood Wide Web," allows plants to share resources like water, carbon, and nutrients. Trees, particularly older, larger ones called "mother trees," can distribute resources to younger seedlings through these networks, helping them grow in less favourable conditions. This decentralised system of resource sharing enhances the survival and health of the entire forest, demonstrating how decentralised networks can support community resilience and development.

Mangrove forests, which thrive in saline coastal waters, exhibit remarkable adaptability and decentralised growth patterns. These trees have evolved unique adaptations, such as aerial roots and salt-filtering systems, allowing them to cope with high salt levels and oxygen-poor soil. Each mangrove tree acts independently to adjust its growth and survival strategies, such as varying root depth and density based on water salinity and soil type. This decentralised adaptation enables mangrove forests to stabilise shorelines, reduce erosion, and support diverse marine life.

Organisations can draw valuable lessons from these natural phenomena by designing systems that mimic these principles of complexity and decentralisation. Instead of rigid hierarchies where decisions flow top-down, companies can implement structures where decision-making is distributed, enabling quicker responses to market changes and internal challenges.

Adopting a holacracy, similar to the self-organising teams seen in nature, can empower employees and promote a more dynamic and resilient organisational structure. For example, a company might create small, autonomous teams responsible for specific projects or goals. Each team operates independently but is interconnected through shared objectives and information networks, much like the interdependent species in an ecosystem.

The Dance of Systems

Managing organisational systems is a delicate dance that requires balancing control with flexibility. Too much control can stifle innovation and adaptability, while too little can lead to chaos and inefficiency. The key is to find the right balance, allowing systems to evolve and adapt while maintaining enough structure to ensure stability and coherence.

Consider the example of a jazz band. While each musician has the freedom to improvise and express their creativity, they must also adhere to certain rules and structures to ensure the performance remains harmonious. This balance between freedom and structure allows the band to create music that is both innovative and cohesive. Similarly, organisations must strike a balance between control and flexibility to thrive in today's complex and dynamic environment.

Navigating the dance floor of organisational systems requires understanding, finesse, and adaptability. By embracing the principles of Catalytic Managership, recognising the Potemkin Village Effect, and designing flexible systems, leaders can create environments that are both resilient and innovative.

The stories of historical figures like Czar Alexander and Mahatma Gandhi, as well as modern examples from the business world, illustrate the importance of these principles in managing complexity.

1. Complexity is not the enemy; it's the dance floor. Learn to waltz, not wrestle. Embrace the intricacies of organisational systems instead of fighting against them. Just like in a dance, understanding the rhythm and flow of complex systems allows you to move gracefully and effectively.

2. True leaders are like gardeners—they cultivate growth rather than command it. Leadership is less about directing every action and more about creating an environment where growth happens naturally. Tend to your organisation like a garden, nurturing potential and removing obstacles.

3. In systems, rigid control is a myth. Flexibility and adaptation are the true superpowers. Attempting to maintain strict control over complex systems often leads to failure. The ability to adapt and be flexible in response to changing circumstances is what truly drives success.

4. The best systems are like sweatpants: comfortable, flexible, and ready for anything. Design organisational systems that are comfortable to operate within and can easily adapt to various situations. Rigid, restrictive systems may look good but often fail under pressure.

5. If your organisation looks perfect on the outside but crumbles inside, you've built a Potemkin village. Avoid creating a facade of success. Ensure that the internal structure and functionality of your organisation are as solid as its outward appearance.

6. The more strings you pull, the more tangled your puppet show becomes. Simplify to amplify. Overcomplicating control mechanisms can lead to chaos. Simplify processes and controls to enhance effectiveness and efficiency.

7. Catalytic leadership isn't about making waves; it's about creating ripples that lead to transformation. Small, strategic actions can

lead to significant changes over time. Focus on facilitating processes rather than forcing outcomes.

8. Effective systems design aligns with natural human behaviours, not against them. Systems should enhance and facilitate natural workflows and behaviours rather than impose rigid structures that go against them.

9. Decentralised power structures foster agility and responsiveness. Distributing decision-making authority helps organisations respond more quickly and effectively to changes and challenges.

10. Innovation thrives in environments where control is balanced with freedom. Creating a balance between control and freedom within an organisation fosters an environment where innovation can flourish.

CHAPTER 07
GO WITH THE GRAIN

The Vector Theory of Systems offers a compelling framework for analysing and understanding the complexities within various systems, whether they are mechanical, biological, or social. At its core, this theory considers each component of a system as a vector, possessing both direction and magnitude. This means every part of the system is not just moving but is moving with a purpose and force that influences the overall system's behaviour and effectiveness.

By employing this theory, we can map out and dissect the various forces at play within any system, visualising how each component's vector contributes to or detracts from the desired system output. It encourages us to look at systems holistically, where each part is interconnected, and their collective movements dictate the system's path. This approach helps in identifying where misalignments occur—where the vectors do not point towards the common goal—allowing for strategic adjustments to ensure that all parts of the system are cohesively aligned and optimised for smooth operation.

Welcome to a journey through the Vector Theory of Systems, where we unravel how systems that groove with human nature aren't just more pleasant—they're also more effective. Imagine a system as a river. When it flows with the natural landscape, it reaches the sea smoothly. But when forced against the terrain, it struggles, twists, and turns, often causing floods. Similarly, when our man-made systems align with the natural currents of human behaviour, they perform seamlessly, enhancing efficiency and effectiveness.

The Automobile: Driving with the Human Vector

Let's kick off with a story of success—the automobile. At the dawn of the 20th century, the car was more than a technological marvel; it was a ticket to freedom. Unlike the horse-drawn carriages that required arduous maintenance and came with their own set of limitations, automobiles promised a new level of autonomy and efficiency. They tapped directly into a profound human desire—the thirst for freedom and control over one's own movements.

The automobile revolution didn't just change how people traveled; it reshaped cities, economies, and cultures. It aligned perfectly with the human vector towards personal empowerment, allowing people to live further from work, thus encouraging the growth of suburbs and expanding the horizons of everyday life. This wasn't just a case of building a better mousetrap; it was about constructing a mousetrap that people didn't even know they needed, and then making it a centrepiece of modern life. Essentially, the car industry didn't just go with the flow—it accelerated it.

Soviet Central Planning: Swimming Against the Current

Now, flip the coin, and you find the Soviet central planning system—a stark contrast to the freewheeling world of automobiles. Imagine a system where instead of harnessing individual desires for achievement and reward, you suppress them under a heavy blanket of collective quotas and centralised control. The Soviet Union's attempt to direct its economy and society through top-down planning was like trying to swim upstream, against the natural human current towards personal success and innovation.

The central planning system often ignored individual motivations, leading to widespread inefficiencies and economic stagnation. Workers and managers, lacking personal incentives, were less likely to innovate or improve productivity. Instead of a bustling marketplace driven by competition and creativity, the Soviet economy was more akin to a congested roundabout, with everyone waiting for directions and no one sure when to go.

This misalignment with human nature showed that even with immense power and resources, fighting the natural human vector is like trying to paddle a canoe with a tennis racket—exhausting and frustratingly ineffective.

Finland's Educational System: Learning in Harmony

Halfway across the world, Finland is turning heads with its educational system, though not through rigorous standardised tests or homework marathons. Instead, Finland focuses on aligning education with the natural curiosity and intrinsic desire for mastery that all students possess. The Finnish educational model is more akin to a guided exploration through a forest of knowledge, rather than a forced march along a predetermined path.

In Finnish schools, there's less emphasis on testing and more on learning through play, inquiry, and real-world application. Teachers are highly trained and given significant autonomy to tailor their teaching to meet students' individual needs and interests. The result? A system where students are not just learning; they're engaged and active participants in their education. This alignment with the natural vectors of human motivation—curiosity and mastery—has made Finland a perennial top performer in international education rankings and has cultivated a generation of students who are not only knowledgeable but also happy and well-adjusted.

The Toyota Production System: Flowing with Efficiency

The Toyota Production System (TPS), also known as lean manufacturing, is an excellent example of a system that leverages natural flows—specifically, the flow of materials and information in manufacturing processes. By eliminating waste through continuous improvement and respecting the human element of manufacturing, TPS aligns with the natural tendencies for efficiency and productivity. This system has not only revolutionised the automotive industry but has also been successfully applied in other sectors, including healthcare and software development.

TPS's focus on "just-in-time" production and "jidoka" (automation with a human touch) ensures that problems are identified and addressed quickly, maintaining a smooth flow of production. By aligning with the human vector for problem-solving and continuous improvement, TPS minimises waste and maximises efficiency.

Southwest Airlines: Point-to-Point Precision

Unlike the traditional hub-and-spoke model used by many airlines, Southwest Airlines employs a point-to-point system that directly connects cities without routing them through a central hub. This system minimises the chances of flight delays and cancellations associated with hub congestion and is naturally aligned with the customer's desire for direct, timely flights. This has contributed significantly to Southwest's reputation for customer satisfaction and operational efficiency.

Southwest's model leverages the vector of customer convenience, reducing unnecessary complexity and enhancing the overall travel experience. By aligning its operational model with the natural human desire for simplicity and efficiency, Southwest has carved out a successful niche in the competitive airline industry.

Buffer's Transparent Salary Formula: Fairness in Action

Buffer, a social media management tool company, uses a transparent salary formula where employees' pay is calculated based on role, experience, and location without any hidden factors. This system aligns with the natural human desire for fairness and transparency, reducing internal conflict and increasing employee satisfaction and trust. By working with the grain of human expectations for fairness, Buffer has created a highly motivated and loyal workforce.

This transparency ensures that employees understand how their compensation is determined, which fosters a sense of equity and trust within the organisation. By aligning with the human vector towards fairness, Buffer has built a company culture that promotes engagement and loyalty.

Amazon Prime: Convenience and Loyalty

Amazon Prime leverages the natural human inclination for convenience and immediacy by offering fast, free shipping, along with a suite of other benefits. This system has been pivotal in cultivating customer loyalty and increasing the frequency and volume of orders. By tapping into the vector of convenience, Amazon has created a service that resonates deeply with customers, driving growth and retention.

The success of Amazon Prime illustrates how aligning a system with fundamental human desires can lead to a significant competitive advantage. By understanding and harnessing the vector of customer convenience, Amazon has built a robust and loyal customer base.

IKEA: Streamlined Simplicity

IKEA's model of selling affordable, flat-pack furniture aligns with the consumer's natural inclination towards convenience and value for money. This system has enabled IKEA to streamline its logistics and offer low prices, driving its global success in the furniture market.

IKEA's approach reduces shipping costs and simplifies storage, while also appealing to customers who appreciate the combination of affordability and practicality. By aligning its business model with the vectors of convenience and cost-effectiveness, IKEA has created a powerful and efficient system.

The U.S. Healthcare System: A Complex Maze

When it comes to the U.S. healthcare system, it often feels like navigating a labyrinth designed by someone who really loved mazes. This complexity is not just a minor inconvenience; it's a fundamental flaw that reflects a deep misalignment with the human need for simplicity and transparency in health management. Patients face a bewildering array of insurance plans, coverage details, and billing codes. Doctors and medical staff spend an increasing amount of time dealing with paperwork and administrative tasks, detracting from the time they could spend on patient care.

This complexity has real consequences: it can lead to delays in treatment, increased costs, and worse health outcomes. The system's inefficiency becomes glaringly apparent when emergencies or pandemics strike, revealing how its complexity hampers rapid response and adaptation. Instead of a streamlined system that helps facilitate care, patients and providers must often fight through red tape just to get the basics done.

Applying the Vector Theory of Systems: Building the Future

The Vector Theory of Systems isn't just a tool for analysing past successes and failures; it's a blueprint for building the future. Whether it's in technology, governance, business, or education, this theory challenges us to rethink how we design systems. It pushes us to consider not just the goals of the system, but the human elements at play—how people interact with, react to, and are influenced by the systems around them.

To design systems that align with the natural vectors of human behaviour, we need to focus on key principles:

1. **Understand Human Motivations:** Systems should be designed with a deep understanding of the intrinsic motivations and desires of the people involved. Whether it's the need for freedom, fairness, efficiency, or convenience, aligning with these motivations is crucial.

2. **Encourage Autonomy and Mastery:** Systems that provide autonomy and opportunities for mastery tend to be more effective. This is evident in Finland's education system and Toyota's production methods, where individuals are empowered to take control and continuously improve.

3. **Simplify and Streamline:** Complexity often leads to inefficiency and frustration. Systems should be as simple and transparent as possible, reducing unnecessary steps and making it easier for people to navigate and interact with them.

4. **Continuous Improvement:** Systems should be designed with flexibility and continuous improvement in mind. This allows them to adapt and evolve in response to changing circumstances and feedback.

5. **Holistic Integration:** Systems should be viewed and designed holistically, considering how each component interacts with and influences the others. This ensures that all parts of the system are working towards the same goals and are cohesively aligned.

Deep insights:

1. **Systems as Living Organisms:** Treat systems like living organisms, where each component's health and direction determine the vitality of the whole. Misalign one element, and the entire system can fall ill.

2. **Freedom as a Catalyst:** The automobile didn't just offer a new way to travel; it redefined freedom, illustrating how systems that unlock human potential can reshape societies.

3. **The Gravity of Human Desire:** Systems that align with human desires, like gravity pulling towards the earth, naturally find the path of least resistance and greatest impact.

4. **Incentives as Compass:** In the maze of Soviet central planning, the absence of personal incentives served as a broken compass, leading the entire system astray.

5. **Curiosity Over Compliance:** Finnish education teaches us that curiosity-driven systems outperform those driven by compliance, suggesting that our natural inquisitiveness is a stronger guide than imposed rules.

6. **The Zen of Lean:** The Toyota Production System embodies a zen-like simplicity and mindfulness, showing how inner clarity and focus on essentials lead to outer efficiency.

7. **Transparency as Trust's Bedrock:** Buffer's transparent salary model demonstrates that trust in systems is built on clear, visible foundations, much like buildings require solid ground.

8. **Convenience as Modern Currency:** Amazon Prime's success underscores that in today's world, convenience is the new currency, valued more than gold.

9. **Simplicity's Hidden Depth:** The U.S. healthcare system's complexity is a testament to the profound power of simplicity, often undervalued until starkly absent.

10. **Systems as Storytellers:** Each system tells a story about its creators and users. The tale of the automobile is one of liberation, while Soviet central planning narrates a cautionary tale of suppression.

CHAPTER 08
FROM DESIGN TO DEVIATION

Imagine you've put together a shiny new toy train set. You've laid out the tracks just so, all according to the grand plan on the box. But when you switch it on, instead of following the tracks, your toy train decides it's more of a cross-country explorer. Off it goes—across the carpet, under the sofa, perhaps taking a dive off the coffee table. Welcome to the world of systems!

Systems, from stock markets to social media platforms, start much like our toy train. They are built with specific tracks to follow—rules, goals, and guidelines designed to ensure they do exactly what we want them to do. But, like our rebellious toy train, systems have a knack for developing minds of their own. Before you know it, they're crafting new paths, often in ways we didn't anticipate or, frankly, even want.

In this chapter, we'll dive into some of the most fascinating stories that will serve as a cautionary tale, a philosophical pondering, and maybe, just a little bit, a comedy of errors scripted by humanity's complex creations.

The Cobra Effect: When Solutions Become Problems

Once upon a time in colonial India, the British officials faced a slithery dilemma that would soon become a serpentine saga. The streets of Delhi were crawling with venomous cobras, which is far from ideal unless you're a snake charmer or a particularly eccentric herpetologist. Concerned for the public's safety the government concocted a plan as straightforward as it was seemingly foolproof.

The solution? A bounty on every dead cobra. Simple, right? Kill a snake, get a reward, reduce the cobra population. It seemed that the British had cracked the code on pest control—until the local entrepreneurial spirit kicked in.

Why risk life and limb hunting dangerous cobras when you can breed them in the safety of your backyard? Before long, the locals started cobra farms (yes, cobra farms), raising the snakes like chickens and then turning them in for a steady profit. Imagine the surprise on the British officials' faces when they realised they were essentially financing a snake-production industry.

Once the officials caught wind of this, they did what any sensible government would do—they scrapped the bounty program. However, the cobra farmers found themselves with a now worthless stock of venomous snakes. Economic rationale being what it is, they did the only logical thing: released the cobras back into the streets. The end result? Delhi had more cobras than before the bounty ever began.

This historical hiccup is a classic example of the "Cobra Effect"—a term coined much later to describe situations where an attempted solution to a problem actually makes the problem worse. It's a stark lesson in the law of unintended consequences, where incentives designed to solve a problem end up encouraging the very behaviour they were meant to curb.

The British attempt to control the cobra population with financial incentives was like trying to put out a fire with gasoline. It turns out that when you pay people per snake, you might just become the unwitting patron of the snake farming industry.

The Cobra Effect teaches us that systems—no matter how well-intentioned—are susceptible to human cleverness and the unpredictability of real-world application. It underscores the need for careful consideration of how people might adapt to and exploit new rules and incentives. After all, when left with a bounty program, some folks will always find a way to breed a bigger problem—literally.

Australia's Cane Toad Catastrophe

Imagine the scene: the lush landscapes of Australia, home to unique wildlife and now, an unexpected guest—the cane toad. Introduced in the 1930s to control pesky cane beetles, these toads were supposed to be the heroes of agriculture. Instead, they hopped right out of the frying pan and into the fire of becoming one of the most notorious ecological blunders in history.

The plan was seemingly simple: release the toads into the sugar cane fields and let them chow down on the beetles threatening the crops. However, someone forgot to check whether the toads could actually reach the beetles, who lived at the tops of the cane stalks, a place no toad had dared to leap before.

With beetles out of reach and the Australian buffet at their disposal, the cane toads did what any self-respecting invasive species would do—they multiplied. Rapidly. With no natural predators to keep their numbers in check, they began a continental tour of Australia, leaving a trail of ecological disruption in their wake.

As they spread, cane toads began impacting native species in devastating ways. Predators, unaccustomed to the toad's toxic skin, died in large numbers after attempting to dine on these new amphibious residents. The toads outcompeted local fauna for food and habitat, tipping the balance of ecosystems that had evolved over millennia without these bulbous invaders.

The cane toad debacle is a textbook example of biological control gone wrong, illustrating a broader lesson in system dynamics. The introduction of the toads was a quick fix to a complex problem, a band-aid solution that ignored the intricate workings of ecological systems. It highlights how interventions can expand beyond their initial boundaries, spiralling into outcomes that are as far-reaching as they are damaging.

This invasive saga serves as a metaphor for any system implemented without full consideration of its broader impacts—economic, technological, or ecological. Like the toads, systems can grow beyond control, their unintended consequences rippling through environments and societies in ways that are difficult, if not impossible, to reverse.

From toads in Australia to tech booms in Silicon Valley, the pattern is clear: interventions in complex systems often lead to outcomes we didn't see coming. The cane toad story reminds us that solving one problem can create another, and sometimes, the cure can be worse than the disease. It's a call to think deeply about the systems we tamper with—because sometimes, those systems hop back in ways we least expect.

Self-Cleaning Paint vs. Graffiti Culture

In the urban jungles of the modern world, graffiti has long been the colourful cry of street artists, splashing city walls with vibrant tags and murals. In response, building owners and city officials, tired of constantly repainting their properties, turned to a futuristic solution: self-cleaning paint. This paint was supposed to end the cycle of graffiti cleanup by making walls that could wash themselves with nothing more than the morning dew or a light rain. But like any good plot twist, this one too had its rebels.

The idea was slick—literally. Walls coated with self-cleaning paint would cause unwanted paint to bead up and roll off, leaving surfaces pristine and tag-free. It seemed like a victory was near for property owners. However, graffiti artists, ever the resourceful lot, saw this not as a deterrent but as a challenge. Enter the era of advanced graffiti.

Innovation in graffiti circles kicked into high gear. Artists began experimenting with new formulations, creating their own versions of super-adhesive sprays that could cling to even the slickest of surfaces. Some concoctions were so potent they could bond to anything from glass to the self-cleaning coatings themselves.

As self-cleaning technology advanced, so did graffiti techniques. What started as a straightforward measure to keep urban aesthetics under control turned into an arms race between paint manufacturers and street artists. Each new generation of self-cleaning paint spurred a counter-innovation in graffiti circles. This back-and-forth battle didn't just push the boundaries of paint technology; it transformed graffiti from mere vandalism into a high-tech game of cat and mouse.

This ongoing war between self-cleaning paint and graffiti artists is a vivid illustration of how technological solutions can inadvertently fuel further innovation on the part of those they're meant to thwart. Instead of quelling graffiti, the technology inspired artists to evolve, much like bacteria developing resistance to antibiotics.

The interaction between self-cleaning paint and graffiti culture highlights a critical aspect of system dynamics: the adaptive nature of human creativity in response to challenges. Just as systems adjust and evolve, so do the behaviours and tactics of those affected by those systems.

The tale of self-cleaning paint and graffiti is more than just an amusing anecdote; it's a lesson in the unpredictability of technological impacts on culture and human behaviour. It reminds us that for every action, there is a reaction, often equal in ingenuity and opposite in intention.

The Unexpected Rise of E-sports

Once upon a time, video games were just arcade entertainment, a way to kill time or procrastinate on homework. Fast-forward to today, and they've morphed into a global competitive phenomenon known as e-sports, packing stadiums, filling live streams, and even affecting international laws. This is a tale of how a leisure activity evolved into a major sporting industry, with all the drama and spectacle of traditional sports.

It all began in the basements and bedrooms, with gamers battling against pixelated foes for high scores. But as technology advanced, so did the complexity and appeal of video games. Multiplayer games took the stage, and with them, informal competitions turned into organised tournaments. What started as fun competitions among friends has exploded into professionally organised events with sponsors, massive audiences, and hefty prize pots.

The rise of e-sports has been meteoric. Games like 'League of Legends,' 'Dota 2,' and 'Overwatch' have become not just pastimes but careers. Players train rigorously, teams strategies with the intensity of football coaches, and the stakes are nothing short of those in any physical sports league.

One of the most striking impacts of e-sports is on the world of broadcasting. Traditional sports channels, which once scoffed at the idea of broadcasting video game tournaments, now vie for broadcasting rights. E-sports events draw millions of viewers online via streaming platforms like Twitch and YouTube, rivalling the viewership of major sporting events like the Super Bowl.

Perhaps one of the most unexpected twists in the rise of e-sports has been its effect on visa legislation. As international tournaments became the norm, players traveling across borders faced legal hurdles. Initially, many were denied entry because their pursuits weren't recognised as legitimate professional endeavours. However, countries like the United States began to grant athlete visas to e-sports players, acknowledging their status as professional athletes and thus changing the very definition of sports and athletes in the eyes of the law.

The transformation of gaming into e-sports highlights a fascinating evolution of systems initially designed for entertainment into complex socio-economic ecosystems. E-sports challenges our traditional notions of what constitutes a sport and what defines an athlete. It has not only expanded the boundaries of entertainment but also forced legal systems, cultural norms, and economic policies to adapt to its rise.

The story of e-sports is a reminder that even the most innocuous or leisurely activities can evolve into serious industries capable of influencing global culture and policy. It shows how systems, when nurtured by passion and innovation, can transcend their original contexts to reshape societies in unexpected ways.

As we've journeyed through tales of cobras, toads, graffiti, and virtual games, it's clear that systems often have minds of their own, deviating from our best-laid plans to chart their own unexpected courses. These stories are not just entertaining anecdotes but vital lessons in the dynamics of systems. They teach us that while we cannot always predict how a system will evolve, we can learn to navigate its surprises with better foresight, flexibility, and a sense of humour.

Identifying Autonomous Systems Through Early Warning Signs

In the complex web of modern systems, spotting when something goes awry early can be crucial to maintaining control and efficiency. Like a detective hunting for clues, observing deviations from expected outcomes can offer the first hint that a system is straying off course. For example, when a social media platform suddenly experiences an unexplained surge in user activity, it might signal an algorithm running amok, pushing content in unforeseen directions. Similarly, robust feedback mechanisms act as a canary in the coal mine. Another telltale sign is systemic resistance—much like when a car resists steering, forcing you to tug harder at the wheel. In organisations, if a new operational policy is met with widespread noncompliance, it might be an indicator that the policy is out of sync with the company's culture or current practices.

Deep insights:

1. **Cobra Clauses:** Never underestimate the creativity of those interacting with your system; a well-meant incentive can sometimes nurture the very problem it seeks to eliminate.

2. **Graffiti Guardrails:** Expect that for every barrier you build, a creative solution to bypass it will emerge—innovation thrives on constraints.

3. **Snakes and Ladders Logic:** Solving one problem may inadvertently create a new one; thorough risk assessment is crucial.

4. **Toad Leap Laws:** Be wary of solutions that seem too simple; they might skip over crucial details that lead to bigger problems.

5. **Game On Governance:** Systems evolve with their users; ensure rules and designs can adapt to emerging trends and strategies.

6. **The Myth of Control:** Recognise that complete control over complex systems is an illusion; prepare for surprises and learn from them.

7. **Incentive Investigation:** Scrutinise every incentive for potential misuse; unintended consequences often stem from well-intentioned rewards.

CHAPTER 09
THE PERFECT ERROR

In the complex landscape of technological development, errors are not merely stumbling blocks but essential components of the innovation process. This chapter explores the intricate dynamics of systems where faults and missteps serve as catalysts for breakthroughs and enhancements. By analysing incidents where anomalies have led to significant advancements, we aim to illustrate the critical role that mistakes play in revealing vulnerabilities, inspiring creative solutions, and refining the overall functionality of systems. As we navigate through a series of case studies, we gain a deeper appreciation for the inherent value of errors in shaping robust and resilient technologies, teaching us to embrace the unexpected as opportunities for progress and ingenuity.

Picture Alexander Fleming, a scientist not unlike many of us, who perhaps didn't always keep the tidiest of workspaces. One day, after a vacation, he returned to a messy lab only to find that one of his Petri dishes, forgotten in the chaos, had become contaminated. But instead of finding just a spoiled sample, Fleming stumbled upon a mould that was aggressively hostile to the surrounding bacteria. This mould, later identified as *Penicillium notatum*, wasn't just any intruder; it was the sort that kicked out the unwanted guests—dangerous bacteria.

This unexpected guest in Fleming's bacterial party turned out to be the jackpot. What was initially an oversight became one of the most celebrated medical breakthroughs: the discovery of penicillin. Fleming's "mould that went gold" didn't just clear up a few bacteria in a dish; it opened the door to treating and curing countless bacterial infections worldwide, saving millions of lives.

This remarkable story highlights a crucial mindset: the brilliance of embracing the unexpected. Fleming could have easily discarded the dish, lamenting his poor lab hygiene. Instead, his curiosity about this strange mould's behaviour led him down a path that revolutionised medicine. It's a profound reminder that sometimes, the best discoveries are the ones we never meant to make. They suggest that serendipity, rather than just sheer pursuit, often holds the key to great scientific leaps. In embracing the accidental, we open ourselves to a world of potential miracles hidden in mishaps.

From Oops to Ops

In the realm of accidental adhesion, the story of Post-it Notes stands out. It all began with Spencer Silver, a chemist at 3M, who was attempting to develop a super-strong adhesive. Instead, he ended up with a weak, repositionable adhesive. This "failure" sat unused for several years until a colleague, Art Fry, was struggling with his bookmarks falling out of his hymnbook. Remembering Silver's adhesive, Fry had a lightbulb moment. He applied some to his bookmarks, and they stuck perfectly—strong enough to hold but weak enough to reposition. Thus, from a botched attempt at creating the ultimate glue, the Post-it Note was born, sticking itself firmly into the annals of great accidental inventions.

Wilson Greatbatch was working on building a device to record heart sounds when he inadvertently installed a wrong resistor. This small blunder caused the device to mimic a human heart's rhythm instead of recording it. Recognising the potential of this serendipitous error, Greatbatch pivoted from his original plan and refined the device into the world's first implantable pacemaker. This device has since saved millions of lives, all thanks to a resistor that was off by just a fraction.

While not a product of an error, the development of wireless LAN technology owes a nod to an office building's quirky architecture, which obstructed wired Internet connections. Dr. John O'Sullivan and his team at CSIRO in Australia were initially trying to detect exploding mini black holes the size of an atomic particle. Although they never found any black holes, their work led to the invention of a key technology used in Wi-Fi, turning architectural frustration into a wireless revolution that changed the way we connect globally.

In 1945, Percy Spencer, an engineer working on radar technology at Raytheon, noticed something unusual while standing near a magnetron, a type of vacuum tube. A chocolate bar in his pocket started melting – more quickly than it would under normal conditions. Curious about this phenomenon, Spencer experimented by placing other food items, like popcorn kernels and an egg, near the magnetron. The popcorn popped, and the egg exploded, leading to his realisation that microwaves could cook food. This accidental discovery led to the development of the microwave oven, revolutionising cooking methods worldwide.

In 1942, while attempting to develop a clear plastic for gun sights during World War II, Dr. Harry Coover discovered a substance that stuck to everything it touched. This substance was initially deemed a failure because it was too sticky to be of practical use for his original purpose. However, nearly six years later, Coover revisited the substance and recognised its potential as a quick-setting adhesive. This led to the commercial development of Super Glue, which became widely used for a variety of applications, from simple household repairs to complex medical uses.

In 1895, Wilhelm Conrad Röntgen, a German physicist, was experimenting with cathode rays, leading to the unexpected discovery of a new kind of ray he called X-rays. While testing whether cathode rays could pass through glass, he noticed a glow coming from a nearby coated screen. Intrigued, he found that these rays could pass through most substances, casting shadows of solid objects. Röntgen's accidental discovery not only earned him the first Nobel Prize in Physics but also revolutionised medical diagnostics by introducing the use of X-rays for scanning the human body.

In 1941, Swiss engineer George de Mestral went for a walk in the woods and noticed how burrs clung to his pants and his dog's fur. Upon examining them under a microscope, de Mestral observed their tiny hooks, which inspired him to create a two-sided fastener: one side with stiff hooks like the burrs and the other with soft loops. After years of development, he successfully patented Velcro, a hook-and-loop fastener that has become a ubiquitous tool in fashion, footwear, space missions, and more.

In 2004, two researchers at the University of Manchester, Andre Geim and Konstantin Novoselov, used a simple piece of Scotch tape to peel off layers from a lump of graphite, a technique stemming from simple curiosity and experimentation. What they managed to create were sheets just one atom thick, later named graphene. This material, discovered almost by accident, has exceptional strength, electrical conductivity, and numerous potential applications, ranging from electronics to composite materials. The discovery was so ground-breaking that it earned them the Nobel Prize in Physics in 2010.

Originally developed in the 1990s by Pfizer as a treatment for high blood pressure and angina, Viagra's potential for treating erectile dysfunction was discovered by accident. During clinical trials, researchers noticed that while the drug wasn't as effective as hoped for heart conditions, many male participants reported improved erections. This led to Viagra being repurposed and marketed as a treatment for erectile dysfunction, becoming one of the most well-known and successful pharmaceuticals in history.

While not a recent discovery, the commercial breakthrough of lithium-ion batteries was significantly influenced by unintended findings. During the 1980s, Akira Yoshino assembled a prototype battery using lithium cobalt oxide and noticed that ions moved between the electrode materials efficiently, something that other researchers had missed. This discovery has had far-reaching implications for mobile phones, electric cars, and many other devices, leading to a Nobel Prize in Chemistry in 2019.

In the world of system development, bugs are often treated like those relatives who show up unannounced at your door—they're rarely welcome, and typically, you want them gone as fast as possible. However, embracing a different perspective on these unexpected "guests" might just change the game. Rather than viewing bugs as merely annoying intrusions, we can consider them as bearers of gifts—those gifts being invaluable lessons and innovative opportunities.

In our journey through the stories of accidental discoveries and fortunate errors, we've seen how what might first appear as mishaps can actually open doors to incredible innovations. Teams that embrace their bugs, instead of merely fixing them, unlock a treasure trove of opportunities. This approach transforms errors from mere annoyances into powerful tools for learning and discovery.

Think about bugs as unseen forces that shape our systems, much like the mysterious dark matter shapes the universe. These bugs might be invisible at first, but they hold immense power to push our systems—and our thinking—to new heights. By diving deep into these bugs, much like Alexander Fleming did with his accidental mould, teams can find surprising insights that lead to big system breakthroughs.

So, let's shift how we view these unexpected guests. Instead of seeing an error and thinking, "Not again!" we can ask, "What's new here?" This simple change in thinking can turn a routine annoyance into an exciting opportunity to learn and innovate. It's about staying curious and open to the unexpected, even when it seems like a setback.

By nurturing this mindset, we don't just prevent future problems; we also create a culture where every mistake has the potential to reveal a new path forward. Let's encourage one another to see the upside in the downs, to learn from every slip-up, and to keep pushing the boundaries of what we think is possible.

So, if you want to whip up better systems, get cozy with your bugs. Study them, embrace them, and yes, fall head over heels for your accidents. Each error, each bug, carries a torch that could light the way to your next big breakthrough.

Deep insights:

1. **Embracing Imperfections in System Design:** In the world of system design, perfection is a moving target, and initial flaws can be invaluable learning opportunities. Encouraging a culture that views imperfections not as failures but as essential steps in the iterative process can lead to more robust and adaptable systems.

2. **Learning from Errors:** Mistakes should be approached with curiosity and as potential opportunities for discovery and innovation. Just as a pirate seeks treasure, system designers and managers should delve into errors to uncover underlying issues and potential improvements that could lead to significant advancements. This mindset helps transform seemingly negative experiences into valuable insights that can pave new pathways to success.

3. **Recycling and Repurposing Ideas:** Innovation isn't always about new creations; sometimes, it's about revisiting and revitalising past ideas that were discarded too soon. Encourage teams to regularly review abandoned projects or previously discarded concepts — these could hold the key to the next breakthrough. This practice not only fosters a culture of sustainability but also encourages creative thinking by looking at old ideas through new lenses.

4. **Documenting and Learning from Mistakes:** Create a systematic approach to archiving errors, blunders, and near-misses within your organisation. This 'Oops Archive' can act as a valuable repository of what not to do, which can be as instructive as guidelines on what to do. By studying past mistakes, teams can avoid future errors and refine their strategies, fostering an environment where continuous learning and adapting from past experiences are part of the organisational DNA.

CHAPTER 10
THE METRIC MISHAP

The Mars Climate Orbiter represented more than just a scientific mission; it was a symbol of human ambition and technological prowess, reaching out to touch another world. NASA set the stage for what was expected to be a breathtaking exploration of our rusty-red neighbour, aiming to study Mars like never before. The excitement was palpable—this was humanity's chance to deepen our understanding of the cosmos.

But here's the twist: with great aspirations come great risks, especially when dealing with the complexities of space travel and robotic explorers. The Mars Climate Orbiter was not just a spacecraft; it was a floating laboratory managed by intricate systems designed to function seamlessly millions of miles from any technician's helping hand. This was no simple task. It's like sending a self-driving car to navigate an obstacle course on the moon—without any roadside assistance.

In this cosmic context, every calculation, every measurement, and every command had to be perfect. A single misstep could (and spoiler alert, did) lead to mission failure. This mission serves as a stark reminder of the razor-thin line between success and failure when managing complex systems, not just in space exploration but in any high-stakes field.

The Mars Climate Orbiter was not just a spaceship; it was a floating dream, designed to do far more than merely orbit a distant planet. The mission had some lofty objectives: to study the Martian climate and atmosphere, provide a comprehensive map of Mars' surface, and serve as a communications relay for subsequent missions. Essentially, it was like planning to set up a high-tech weather station on Mars, complete with its own satellite dish to phone home the data.

To achieve these ambitious goals, NASA and its contractors, including Lockheed Martin, developed a sophisticated technological setup:

- **Spacecraft Design:** The Mars Climate Orbiter itself was equipped with the latest in space technology, from solar panels for power to high-tech instruments for gathering all sorts of scientific data.

- **Navigation and Communication Systems:** Precision instruments and communication systems were installed to ensure it could navigate correctly around Mars and send data back to Earth. This setup was supposed to be the ultimate in long-distance call technology.

- **Collaborative Framework:** The project was a massive collaborative effort involving multiple teams across different organisations. NASA provided the mission oversight and scientific objectives, while Lockheed Martin handled much of the engineering and spacecraft construction.

The organisational structure was meticulously designed to ensure seamless integration between the different teams. There was a clear hierarchy and protocol for nearly every process, from system checks to data handling. In theory, it was a well-oiled machine, with each cog in the system interlocking neatly with the next.

However, as with any grand plan, the devil was in the details—or, more precisely, in the units of measurement, which would soon prove to be a critical oversight. This initial setup, while impressive on paper, set the stage for one of the most educational missteps in space exploration history. It's a stark reminder that even the most advanced systems need to double-check the basics, like ensuring everyone is quite literally speaking the same language—or in this case, using the same measurements.

The Mars Climate Orbiter incident serves as a classic example of a small oversight leading to a colossal setback, showcasing the critical importance of alignment in collaborative projects. This particular misstep involved a simple yet fatal error: the confusion between metric and imperial units.

NASA, as an institution steeped in scientific tradition, naturally used the metric system—the choice of scientists worldwide. Meanwhile, Lockheed Martin, one of NASA's key contractors, operated using the imperial system, which is prevalent in the United States but not in international scientific endeavours. This difference might seem trivial to the layperson, akin to deciding whether to measure ingredients in a recipe in cups or grams. However, in the precision-driven realm of space exploration, this was more like using cups when a precise gram count was necessary for the perfect chemical reaction.

The mix-up came down to one team calculating the force of the spacecraft's thrusters in pounds (imperial), while another team assumed the measurements were in newtons (metric). This critical miscommunication meant that every manoeuvre made by the orbiter was off-target.

Imagine a large corporation where one department sets a budget in U.S. dollars, while another department, perhaps based in a different country, mistakenly operates under the assumption that the budget is in euros. The seemingly minor confusion about currency could lead to significant overspending or underspending, much like the trajectory error experienced by the Mars Climate Orbiter.

In the case of the Mars Climate Orbiter, this misalignment led to the spacecraft approaching Mars at a dangerously low altitude, far closer than intended. The orbiter was supposed to stabilise at a safe orbital distance to function as a climate observer and communication relay. Instead, it dipped into the Martian atmosphere, where it quickly disintegrated due to the intense heat—a mistake that burned up a $327 million investment.

This incident starkly illustrates how vital it is to ensure clear, unambiguous communication in any system, especially one involving diverse teams or intricate technologies. It wasn't just a spacecraft that was lost, but years of planning, resources, and the potential for significant scientific discoveries. In any corporate or technical environment, ensuring that all team members and systems "speak the same language" can be the difference between soaring success and a disastrous crash.

The immediate aftermath of the spacecraft's destruction was a mix of shock and disbelief. For NASA, this was a failure that went beyond mere financial loss; it was a significant setback to its Mars exploration agenda. The orbiter was not only tasked with studying the Martian climate but also intended to serve as a vital communications relay for future missions. Its loss meant a delay in numerous planned activities and projects that depended on its data and relay capabilities. The scientific community felt the ripple effects, as several key studies and experiments were put on hold or canceled.

Publicly, NASA's reputation took a hit. The error led to widespread criticism over what many saw as a basic and avoidable mistake. For an organisation that prides itself on precision and advanced technological capabilities, the mix-up between metric and imperial units was an embarrassing blunder. It raised questions about NASA's internal practices and project management skills, casting a shadow over its competency. Critics and the media had a field day, and the incident became fodder for comedians and satirists, further tarnishing NASA's image.

Strategically, the loss of the Mars Climate Orbiter forced NASA to reevaluate and revamp its procedures and protocols. It led to an increased emphasis on cross-verification and double-checking of data, especially when collaborating with external contractors. The disaster underscored the need for stringent oversight and comprehensive communication protocols across all levels of a mission.

The incident also prompted a broader discussion within the space exploration community about risk management and error mitigation strategies. It became a case study on the importance of cohesive system integration and the dangers of compartmentalisation in project management.

The Mars Climate Orbiter disaster serves as a stark reminder that misalignments can have drastic consequences, not just in space exploration but across various domains. This section examines how similar misalignments have led to notable failures in the business world, particularly with international expansions where understanding and integrating local practices are crucial.

Home Depot's venture into China is a textbook example of strategic misalignment with local culture. The American giant stepped into the Chinese market with its successful do-it-yourself (DIY) model, expecting it to resonate with Chinese consumers. However, DIY culture isn't as prevalent in China, where labor is affordable and the concept of self-assembled furniture or home repairs is not part of the norm. Chinese consumers prefer buying finished products or hiring professionals to manage home improvement projects. Despite converting some of their locations to more localised formats, Home Depot failed to grasp the fundamental cultural preferences, leading to the closure of all their mainland stores in 2012. This misstep was akin to using imperial units in a metric world; the basic assumptions about the market were off.

Starbucks' struggle in Australia offers another example of a misalignment with local expectations. When Starbucks entered the Australian market, it banked on its global brand appeal and standard coffee menu to attract customers. However, Australia has a strong, unique coffee culture with an emphasis on local cafés and high-quality, artisan coffee. The generic Starbucks experience didn't appeal to Australian coffee aficionados, who found the coffee below their usual standard and the atmosphere lacking the local café charm. Starbucks failed to adapt its offerings to the sophisticated tastes of the Australian market, leading to a significant scale-back and closure of numerous outlets. This scenario mirrors the Mars Orbiter's failure, where assumptions based on familiar settings led to adverse outcomes in a different environment.

These examples highlight a crucial point: the importance of aligning strategies with the local context. Whether it's entering a new market or launching a space mission, understanding and integrating the specific conditions and requirements of the target environment is crucial. The consequences of overlooking these can be costly, as seen with NASA, Home Depot, and Starbucks.

Just as NASA learned the hard way, companies must realise that precision in understanding and catering to local markets is equally vital. The key takeaway is to conduct thorough market research, foster local partnerships, and adapt strategies to meet local preferences and practices. This approach can help avoid the pitfalls of misalignment and set the stage for success in any venture, terrestrial or otherwise.

By learning from these missteps, organisations can better navigate the complexities of entering new domains, ensuring they are not just transplanting a one-size-fits-all strategy but are truly adapting to meet diverse and nuanced needs.

Designing systems that are both effective and resilient requires more than just good intentions; it demands a set of principles that are as practical as they are insightful. Below are some enhanced, actionable principles and thumb rules that add depth and specificity to the task of creating fault-tolerant systems:

Principle of Contextual Standardisation: Adapt While You Align

Rather than simply enforcing uniform standards, adapt these standards to fit the context of each unit or division while maintaining alignment with the overall mission. Think of it like a jazz band—while there's a common tune everyone follows, each musician adjusts their play to resonate with the venue and the audience, ensuring harmony without losing individual expression. This principle advocates for a flexible standardisation that respects and integrates local variations, enhancing both local relevance and systemic coherence.

Principle of Proactive Verification: Trust, but Verify Ahead

Instead of periodic verifications, integrate continuous, proactive checks throughout the lifecycle of a project. Use predictive analytics and real-time data to anticipate discrepancies before they evolve into problems. Imagine this as the GPS navigation of system management—constantly recalculating the route based on traffic data (real-time feedback), rather than waiting for a missed turn to realise an update is needed.

Principle of Multidirectional Communication: Create Feedback Loops

Expand the principle of transparent communication by establishing multidirectional feedback loops that allow information to flow in multiple directions—from the ground up and back down again. This is akin to having not just a suggestion box but a town hall where ideas and feedback are actively discussed and integrated. It ensures that every layer of the organisation is both a contributor and a recipient of vital information, fostering a culture of open communication and continuous adaptation.

Principle of Strategic Failure Analysis: Learn Strategically, Not Just Systematically

Beyond systematically analysing failures, focus on strategic learning—identify patterns and root causes, and apply these insights to strengthen future planning and execution. Think of it as a detective solving a case, not just by looking at what went wrong, but by understanding why it went wrong and how similar issues can be prevented. This principle involves transforming every mishap into a learning opportunity that informs strategic decisions, turning setbacks into stepping stones for innovation.

By adopting these refined principles, organisations can design systems that are not only robust and fault-tolerant but also dynamic and adaptive. These guidelines help navigate the complexities of modern systems, ensuring they are prepared to meet challenges head-on and turn potential failures into opportunities for growth and improvement. This approach doesn't just patch vulnerabilities—it enhances the system's overall resilience and efficacy, paving the way for long-term success.

The tale of the Mars Climate Orbiter isn't just a story about a spacecraft; it's a universal saga of what happens when attention to detail takes a backseat on the bus of grand ambitions. This incident serves as a cautionary tale reminding us that whether you're sending a robot to Mars or just trying to coordinate a Monday morning meeting, the devil really is in the details.

Here's the kicker: every field, whether it's healthcare, finance, technology, or even baking, has its own version of the Mars Climate Orbiter waiting to happen if we're not careful. In baking, confuse teaspoons with tablespoons, and your fluffy cake becomes a kitchen calamity. In finance, a misplaced decimal could mean the difference between a bonus and a blow-up.

Leadership in every sector needs to champion this cause, ensuring that teams have the tools, training, and time to focus on the details that matter. It's about creating environments where asking, "Could this be our Mars Climate Orbiter moment?" is a sign of strategic thinking, not skepticism.'

As we reflect on the story of the Mars Climate Orbiter, let it inspire us not just to plan with precision but to execute with exactitude. Let's turn this cautionary tale into a playbook for precision that we apply to our projects, ensuring that when we shoot for the stars—be it literally or metaphorically—we don't miss and burn up in the atmosphere of oversight.

Deep insights:

1. **Precision as a Core Value**: The Mars Climate Orbiter's failure underscores the critical nature of precision in system operations, particularly in high-stakes environments. This extends beyond space missions to any field where precise measurements and strict adherence to standards are necessary. Emphasising precision as a core organisational value can prevent costly errors, promoting a culture where meticulous attention to detail is the norm, not the exception.

2. **Harmonisation of Standards**: The incident highlights the importance of standardising units of measurement and protocols across all teams and partners. In a globalised world, the harmonisation of standards across international borders and between different sectors can facilitate smoother operations and prevent misunderstandings that lead to failure.

3. **Integrated Systems Thinking**: The oversight in the Mars Orbiter mission was partly due to a lack of integrated systems thinking, where different components of the project were handled by teams operating in silos. Developing a systems thinking approach can help identify potential points of failure where critical information may be lost or misinterpreted.

4. **Risk Management through Redundancy**: Incorporating redundancy in critical measurements and operations can serve as a fail-safe against human error. This means not just double-checking but having multiple, independent checks on important data and decisions, much like the aviation industry's use of redundant systems to ensure safety.

CHAPTER 11

GROWTH UNCHECKED

Imagine acquiring a small pet dragon, initially charming and manageable, that slowly grows into a behemoth beyond your control. At first, it might light your fireplace, but as it grows, it could set the entire house ablaze. This reflects the nature of expansive systems within organisations—they start as manageable solutions but can grow into uncontrollable forces consuming vast resources.

Organisations often start with simple, effective systems that solve specific problems. However, as these systems grow and evolve, they can become overly complex and difficult to manage. This unchecked growth can create inefficiencies and unintended consequences, much like a pet dragon growing into a dangerous beast. Leaders must be vigilant in monitoring and managing the growth of their systems to ensure they remain effective and do not become unwieldy.

In the world of systems—whether they're made up of people, tech, or trees—growth is just as sure a thing as Monday morning blues. Systems stretch and sprawl like vines, driven by human dreams and sheer necessity. But just like unchecked vines can strangle a tree, unchecked growth in systems can turn into a bit of a monster, complicating things and setting traps for itself.

Let's break it down: systems have a natural tendency to grow, kind of like how your collection of stuff accumulates until you can't ignore the clutter. It's not always because someone made a bad plan; it's just what systems do. They grow whether they're shiny tech networks, government bureaucracies, or your weekly grocery list.

In this chapter, we're diving into why and how systems keep growing, linking it to our big theme—when systems fail, sometimes it's because they've grown too big. Unchecked growth can spin a tangled web of problems, turning a system's success into its own worst enemy. Without some smart control, growth doesn't just mean getting bigger and better; it might also mean heading for a crash.

We'll explore the rules that seem to dictate how systems expand, pulling in lessons from history and the latest insights to show the good, the bad, and the ugly of growth. Plus, we'll look at ways to handle this growth smartly, so our systems can get bigger without getting messier. This chat isn't just academic—it's about giving you the tools to see the growth coming and handle it like a pro, whether you're running a startup, a city council, or just trying to keep your email inbox from exploding.

Parkinson's Law

Here's a funny truth about work: it's like gas. No, not the kind you need to avoid in elevators. We're talking about how work expands to fill whatever time you give it. Cyril Northcote Parkinson, a keen observer of the British Civil Service, noted this phenomenon when he saw bureaucracies bloating over time, with no real increase in the actual amount of work.

Imagine you need to organise a weekly meeting agenda. Sounds like a half-hour job, right? But if your boss gives you half a day to do it, suddenly, that agenda becomes a multi-page document, complete with colour-coded sections and maybe even a pre-meeting to discuss the meeting. Why? Just because the extra time is there!

Big-Bang Theorem of Systems-Cosmology

No telescopes needed here—we're looking at how systems grow just like the universe does, endlessly and often unnecessarily.

Think about the last time you used a simple app on your phone, maybe something as straightforward as an email app. Initially, it was all about sending emails, right? Then came updates: now it can schedule meetings, manage tasks, integrate social feeds. Each new feature is like a new star in the cosmos of that app, making it bulkier and sometimes slower than when it was just a simple email app.

Parkinson's Extended Law

Building on the original law, Parkinson threw some math into the mix. He suggested that systems naturally expand by about 5-6% each year, whether they need to or not. It's like your system has a mind of its own, deciding it's going to grow regardless of the actual work demand. Here's an easy way to see this in action: look at a city's public transportation plan. Imagine the city decides to add more buses or extend routes by 5% each year because, well, that's the plan. But if the number of riders doesn't actually increase, you end up with more buses roaming half-empty, burning fuel and budget, and not really helping anyone get around more efficiently.

These concepts are real patterns that can lead to inefficiency and resource wastage. By understanding them, we can better manage growth, making sure our systems and projects stay lean, mean, and effective, rather than turning into sprawling galaxies of complexity.

The Roman Empire: Over-expansion and Its Pitfalls

Consider the Roman Empire, which experienced tremendous growth that brought wealth and expanded its territories significantly. This expansion seemed beneficial initially, as it brought more resources and influence. However, managing such a vast empire proved challenging. Governance stretched thin, and the military found itself overextended. The need to control distant territories introduced complex new administrative systems, which eventually led to inefficiencies and widespread corruption. This over-expansion weakened the empire internally, contributing significantly to its eventual decline. The story of Rome is a classic example of how rapid expansion without solid control mechanisms can lead to systemic inefficiencies and failures.

Amazon Web Services (AWS)

Turning to the tech world, Amazon Web Services (AWS) shows how a system can expand rapidly yet maintain high levels of efficiency. AWS began as a modest part of Amazon offering basic services to small businesses but grew to become a crucial component of the internet infrastructure. Despite its massive growth, AWS managed to avoid the pitfalls of expansion through careful architectural planning and a focus on modular services. This approach allows customers to utilise just what they need without being overwhelmed. Unlike many tech platforms that struggle under their own complexity, AWS has continued to thrive, supporting vast enterprises without sacrificing service quality.

These case studies illustrate two sides of systemic growth. While growth can enhance power and resources, if not managed carefully, it can lead to significant challenges and potentially jeopardise a system's integrity and functionality. The Roman Empire shows the risks of expanding faster than management capacity allows, while AWS demonstrates that with careful planning and adaptability, even vast systems can remain efficient and service-oriented. These lessons emphasise the importance of strategic oversight and modular planning in managing growth effectively.

Unpacking the Growth Machine

The Internal Forces: Complexity in the Pursuit of Efficiency

Companies grow like ambitious gardeners planting new seeds, aiming for more control, smoother operations, or a bigger market share. They introduce new tools or create departments to boost productivity and outpace competition. However, these additions often complicate rather than simplify. It's like upgrading a simple toaster to a multifunctional device that also fries eggs and brews coffee—great in theory, but overwhelming when you just want toast. The irony is that efforts to streamline and simplify can often lead to increased complexity, trapping efficiency in a web of bureaucracy.

The External Forces: Navigating the World's Curveballs

External pressures also shape system complexity. Think of the system as a boat. Smooth sailing is easy in calm waters, but regulatory storms or competitive speedboats can force you to add bigger engines or more sails just to keep up. For example, banks have expanded their compliance teams to meet new financial regulations—a necessary move that also adds operational complexity.

And then there's technology. It's like a race where everyone is trying to be the fastest with the newest gadgets. Companies scramble to integrate the latest tech to stay relevant and competitive, but this race can lead to hastily slapped-on tech solutions that don't always play nice with the existing systems.

The Balancing Act: Growing Smart, Not Just Big

As these internal ambitions and external pressures build up, systems reach a tipping point. Beyond this point, more growth doesn't mean better performance; it might just mean more headaches. It's crucial to understand how to expand without tripping over our own feet. This isn't just about growth—it's about smart growth, managing the complexities so that they don't mutate our strengths into weaknesses.

Efficiency Loss: When More Becomes Less

Imagine a tech company that's expanding fast. They're hiring, they're acquiring, and they're piling on new projects. Initially, it feels like progress—it's buzzing, it's exciting. But as they grow, things start to get muddy. The clear communication paths and quick decision-making that once made them agile now turn into a messy game of corporate telephone, where messages get lost or distorted along the way. What started as a sprint becomes a clumsy three-legged race, tripping over its own growth.

Vulnerability Increase: When Bigger Isn't Better

A larger system doesn't just mean more resources; it means a bigger target for problems. Think of it as a giant spaceship—more engines, more control panels, and more places where things can go wrong. A growing company might face new security threats, and every new software patch or system integration can open doors to new vulnerabilities. It's like expanding a fortress but having more doors to guard.

And as the system grows, keeping an eye on everything becomes tougher. Responsibilities are spread thin over more people and more departments, making it hard to spot where problems start. It's like trying to find a needle in a haystack, but the haystack is growing every day.

Mastering the Growth Game

Wrapping up our journey into the world of system expansion, it's clear that smart growth isn't just nice to have—it's essential for the vitality of any organisation. We've traveled through the natural tendencies of systems to stretch their limbs, motivated by inner dreams and outer demands. And we've seen how, without a careful eye, this growth can twist into a tangle of inefficiencies and vulnerabilities.

Whether you're dealing with tech systems, company structures, or community networks, think about how you can make them not just bigger, but better and more resilient. Don't just watch your systems grow—guide them. Steer your projects towards sustainable expansion and enduring strength.

Deep insights:

1. **The Complexity Paradox:** Like a garden that needs regular pruning to avoid becoming an overgrown jungle, organisations must streamline their processes as they grow. This helps prevent the blooming complexity from choking productivity. Keeping growth in check ensures that a system remains functional and efficient, just like careful gardening keeps plants healthy and pleasing to the eye.

2. **The Law of Diminishing Returns:** There's a point in every system's growth—be it a business or a bureaucracy—where adding more starts to give you less back. It's like stuffing more clothes into an already full drawer; eventually, it becomes hard to close. Recognising when enough is enough helps maintain a healthy balance and avoids the burdens that come with excessive expansion.

3. **Entropy in Organisations:** Just as a room gets messier without regular tidying, companies can descend into chaos as they expand unless efforts are made to maintain clarity and order. Injecting energy through clear leadership, open communication, and consistent training ensures that growth doesn't lead to disarray.

4. **The Ecosystem Analogy:** Think of a business like a forest ecosystem where balance is key. Just as the unchecked growth of a particular species can disrupt an entire ecosystem, unchecked growth in a company can cause significant disruptions.

5. **Strategic Saturation:** Like a sponge that can only soak up so much water, a company has limits to how much change it can effectively absorb at once. Recognising these limits prevents the 'spillover' effects of inefficiencies or redundancies that can occur when new teams or technologies overwhelm existing structures.

CHAPTER 12
SYSTEMIC RESISTANCE

Welcome to the world of systems, where the battle between theoretical efficiency and practical challenges plays out on a grand stage. This dynamic is perfectly illustrated by Le Chatelier's Principle, a concept from chemistry that explains how systems resist changes to their equilibrium. While originally applied to chemical reactions, this principle offers a profound metaphor for understanding broader organisational and systemic behaviours.

Imagine trying to push a giant spring into a smaller box. The more you push, the harder the spring pushes back. This is similar to how systems behave when changes are introduced. Whether in chemistry, physics, or organisational systems, there's an inherent resistance to change, a desire to maintain the status quo, even when change is necessary for progress.

This chapter sets the stage for a broader discussion on the irony of system design. Systems are often crafted with the intent to streamline operations, enhance efficiency, and simplify processes. Yet, paradoxically, these systems frequently end up complicating the very issues they were designed to resolve. Layers of bureaucracy, misalignments of objectives and practices, and cumbersome protocols can turn what should be a streamlined process into a labyrinth of inefficiency.

The Characters: Satguru and Mr. Smith

Meet Satguru, a project manager with a passion for sustainable business practices, working at EcoInnovate, a company known for its green technologies. Ideally, Satguru's role would involve developing new initiatives and strategies to enhance the company's sustainability footprint. However, he frequently encounters a significant mismatch between his innovative objectives and the suffocating bureaucratic demands of his corporate environment.

Satguru is an energetic professional who thrives on turning eco-friendly theories into actionable business strategies. His enthusiasm for pushing the envelope in sustainable practices is often dampened by the dense layers of corporate bureaucracy imposed by his upper management, particularly his department head, Mr. Hawthorn. Known for his conservative approach, Mr. Hawthorn prefers meticulous planning and exhaustive documentation over agile execution.

Mr. Hawthorn recently championed a new operational framework called the "Strategic Alignment System." This system requires all project managers to submit detailed quarterly reports outlining their project goals, resources, anticipated outcomes, and alignment with the company's long-term strategic objectives. For Satguru, this means his dynamic role is reduced to a series of endless planning and reporting cycles. Each project initiative must now navigate a gauntlet of pre-approvals, risk assessments, and compliance checks before any actual work can begin. Satguru finds himself spending more time justifying his sustainability projects to various internal committees than implementing them. The requirement to continually align his innovative projects with the rigid structures of the Strategic Alignment System stifles his ability to act swiftly on emerging opportunities in the green technology sector.

This constant dance with bureaucracy would be laughable if it weren't so counterproductive. Satguru, hired for his ability to innovate and drive change, finds himself entangled in procedural red tape. Instead of leading his team towards cutting-edge sustainable solutions, he is bogged down by the need to produce voluminous documentation and navigate the political maze of corporate approval processes. His predicament reflects a common dysfunction in many large corporations where the process often overshadows purpose. Systems designed to ensure control and minimise risk can inadvertently suppress the agility and creativity needed to stay ahead in fast-moving industries like green technology.

Satguru's experience highlights the critical need for corporations to balance oversight with empowerment. In the quest to manage risks and maintain control, companies must be careful not to choke the innovation that drives their business forward. Leaders should strive to create systems that facilitate rather than frustrate, removing unnecessary bureaucratic hurdles and fostering an environment where innovative ideas can thrive.

Corporate systems should be designed to support strategic agility and operational efficiency, allowing project managers like Satguru to execute their initiatives with fewer impediments. By reducing bureaucratic overhead and empowering employees to make decisions at the local level, companies can enhance their responsiveness and competitive edge in the marketplace. This approach not only accelerates project timelines but also boosts morale and retains high-caliber talent, turning potential bureaucratic nightmares into ecosystems of innovation and success.

Now meet Mr. Smith, once the beloved mentor at EcoInnovate, known for his sage advice and the uncanny ability to spark brilliant ideas over a cup of coffee. His transition from a wise guru to a rigid gatekeeper mirrors a familiar tale of transformation under the weight of corporate red tape.

In the beginning, Mr. Smith was more than just a manager; he was the creative spark-plug of EcoInnovate. He wandered around the office, tossing out challenging questions and encouraging debates that often led to breakthrough ideas. However, as the winds of corporate mandates blew stronger, demanding tighter controls and exhaustive reporting, Mr. Smith's role began to shift. Tasked with enforcing the new Strategic Alignment System, he transformed from the team's cheerleader to the chief compliance officer.

Now, he spends his days not brainstorming over coffee but poring over spreadsheets, ensuring every project ticks all the right boxes in corporate checklists. The transition from being an idea cultivator to a rule enforcer is stark, turning him into the very embodiment of the bureaucratic drag he once cleverly navigated.

This change has rippled across the team. The lively, impromptu brainstorms that defined EcoInnovate's culture are now replaced with meetings dominated by compliance updates and risk avoidance tactics. The office that once buzzed with energy now ticks to the mundane rhythm of checkboxes and approvals. Mr. Smith, once the team's guiding light, now casts a long shadow over creative spirits, often extinguishing the innovative flames he used to fuel.

Morale has taken a hit, too. The team, previously vibrant and collaborative, now operates in silos, mechanically pushing towards predefined, often uninspired targets. The shift in atmosphere is palpable, turning what was once a dynamic workshop of ideas into a factory line of efficiency—a place where innovation is not about 'what could be' but rather 'what must be.'

Mr. Smith's journey from a guru to a gatekeeper highlights the delicate balance between maintaining control and fostering creativity. It serves as a humorous yet poignant reminder that when companies saddle their brightest minds with too much bureaucracy, they risk dimming the very innovations that light their path to success.

For companies aiming to stay ahead of the curve, it's crucial to design systems that allow leaders like Mr. Smith to nurture creativity while keeping the ship steady. This balance is essential for cultivating an environment where innovation thrives under the guidance of wisdom, not drowned by the weight of paperwork.

Misaligned Feedback Mechanisms: The Double-Edged Sword

Feedback mechanisms in any system are like the spices in cooking—they can make or break the dish. In an ideal world, feedback helps systems self-correct, improve continuously, and stay aligned with their goals. It's supposed to work like a well-tuned GPS, guiding the system back on course whenever it starts to drift off the intended path.

Feedback loops are the silent heroes of system regulation, providing the necessary input to refine processes and outputs continuously. Imagine a thermostat in your home—it measures the temperature and adjusts the heating or cooling to maintain your set comfort level. Similarly, in a corporate setting, feedback should help departments adjust their strategies and operations to better meet company goals.

However, when feedback mechanisms go awry, they can do more harm than good. Take the case of Mr. Smith and his team at EcoInnovate. Initially, feedback was intended to foster innovation and guide the team toward sustainable practices. But with the introduction of overly stringent compliance measures, feedback started to feel more like a straightjacket than guidance.

For instance, if a tech company starts rewarding programmers for the number of code commits rather than the quality of their work, it creates a coding frenzy. Programmers might start churning out lines of code like a factory conveyor belt, prioritising quantity over quality. It's like a chef who's told the more dishes he cooks, the better, regardless of how they taste—resulting in a lot of unpalatable meals.

On the flip side, positive feedback, when not properly calibrated, can lead to what's known as runaway processes. Imagine a scenario where every minor success in a project gets overly celebrated, creating a false sense of progress. It's akin to giving a child a trophy for every little scribble—they might end up thinking they're the next Picasso, when in fact, they're not quite there yet.

In Mr. Smith's department, this kind of feedback led to a cycle where the mere completion of compliance forms was seen as a significant achievement. This misplaced focus diverted attention from real, substantive outcomes, like advancing sustainable technologies. The department became a place where ticking off checkboxes was celebrated more than actual innovation, creating a bubble of inefficiency that looked impressive on the outside but was hollow at the core.

Feedback, while essential, is a double-edged sword that must be wielded with precision and care. In Mr. Smith's case, the feedback mechanisms that were supposed to drive the department forward ended up either stifling creativity or inflating inefficiencies. The lesson here is clear: like adding just the right amount of spice to a dish, feedback in any system needs to be carefully balanced to truly enhance performance and foster an environment where real growth can occur.

Systemic Inertia and the Perpetual Loop

Systemic inertia often traps organisations in a continuous loop of action without progress, akin to being stuck on a treadmill—running hard but staying in the same place.

Imagine a committee tasked with improving productivity. They meet regularly, each time proposing new initiatives or slightly altered versions of old plans. Yet, every proposal is met with "further review," "more data needed," or gets shelved for the next big idea. It's a bit like a dog chasing its tail—lots of energy expended but no forward progress. This cycle can become so entrenched that it turns into a comfort zone, where the fear of actual change keeps the organisation in a state of motion without movement.

For Mr. Smith and his team at EcoInnovate, systemic inertia has led to a frustrating cycle of redundancy. Every quarter, the team drafts extensive reports and action plans. However, instead of implementing these plans and iterating based on results, they find themselves revising and expanding the documents to meet ever-changing guidelines and benchmarks set by upper management. It's akin to preparing for a marathon but never actually running it; instead, they keep buying new running shoes.

This phenomenon is not unique to Mr. Smith's team or even to private corporations; it's pervasive in many large organisations, including government entities. Here, systemic inertia can lead to significant human costs. For example, consider a government agency responsible for public health initiatives. When bogged down by bureaucratic inertia, critical health programs might be delayed or watered down, directly impacting community well-being. Each "pending review" or "additional approval" can translate to real delays in addressing public health crises, where time is often of the essence.

In large corporations, the human cost manifests as job dissatisfaction, decreased productivity, and a dampened spirit of innovation among employees. Workers become disenchanted, feeling that their efforts are futile, which can lead to high turnover rates and a loss of talented individuals who seek more dynamic and impactful environments.

Breaking out of systemic inertia requires a deliberate shift in organisational culture and processes. It demands leadership that is willing to cut through the bureaucratic tape, streamline decision-making processes, and commit to seeing initiatives through to their conclusion. Leaders must foster an environment where iterative action is valued over perpetual planning, and where moving forward, even with some risk, is preferred over stagnation.

For Mr. Smith and similar leaders, the challenge is to transform their organisations from being like a carousel, which spins predictably in circles, to more like a rollercoaster—where there are ups and downs, but at least it's moving forward, bringing excitement and real experiences. This shift is crucial not just for the health of the organisation but for the well-being and engagement of everyone involved.

Deep insights:

1. **The Resilience Paradox**: Much like Le Chatelier's Principle in chemistry, where systems resist changes to return to equilibrium, organisational systems often inherently resist changes that could lead to efficiency. This paradoxical resistance can be visualised as a spring that, when compressed (changed), pushes back to regain its original shape. Understanding this dynamic is crucial for effectively implementing change that is sustainable and minimally disruptive.

2. **Bureaucratic Entropy**: In the universe of organisational systems, entropy increases as bureaucracy expands, often leading to disorder and inefficiency rather than the intended order. Each layer of bureaucracy potentially dilutes the impact of actions meant to streamline processes. Leaders need to be vigilant about the entropic effects of bureaucracy—simplifying where possible to enhance system responsiveness and agility.

3. **Cultural Inertia**: Cultural inertia within organisations acts as a hidden force that resists change, similar to physical inertia which resists changes in motion. This inertia can be deeply embedded in corporate culture, manifesting as "this is how we've always done it" attitudes. Overcoming this requires significant energy and effort, with a focused push towards fostering a culture that values adaptability and continuous improvement.

4. **Feedback Fidelity**: Just as feedback mechanisms in mechanical systems help maintain stability, feedback in organisational systems is essential for alignment with strategic objectives. However, if feedback loops are flawed or misaligned, they can exacerbate existing problems rather than resolve them. High fidelity in feedback mechanisms ensures that the system remains responsive and adjustments are timely and effective.

5. **Systemic Adaptation vs. Adoption**: There's a subtle yet profound difference between adapting a system to meet new needs

and adopting new systems altogether. Effective system management often requires adaptation—tweaking and refining existing systems to improve function without overhauling the entire structure, thereby minimising disruption and resistance.

6. **Simplicity in Complexity**: One of the greatest challenges in system design is achieving simplicity on the other side of complexity. This means designing systems that are easy to use and understand, despite the complex functions they perform. Achieving this can significantly enhance system usability and effectiveness, reducing resistance to usage and increasing overall system performance.

CHAPTER 13
SLACK IN SYSTEM DESIGN

Welcome to the fascinating world of system design, where the pursuit of peak efficiency often feels like walking a tightrope. On one side, sleek, streamlined systems promise ultimate performance with minimal waste. On the other, there's the harsh reality: these perfect systems can crumble under the slightest unexpected pressure. This chapter explores a critical paradox: the quest for total efficiency often conflicts with the need for systems to be durable and adaptable in the face of real-world chaos. We'll uncover why more flexible systems, which might seem inefficient at first glance, can outperform their highly tuned counterparts over time.

Imagine a system as a high-performance race car, engineered to excel under perfect conditions. Now, picture this car navigating a pothole-filled city street—it's a recipe for disaster. This scenario illustrates what happens when systems designed for maximum efficiency encounter the unexpected; they can shatter like glass.

Consider our modern electrical grids. These marvels of engineering are designed to manage specific loads with minimal waste, epitomising efficiency. Yet, when an unexpected storm hits or demand spikes suddenly, these grids can fail spectacularly. Large-scale blackouts often begin with a minor glitch but spread rapidly, leaving millions in the dark. The grid's efficiency means there's no cushion, no slack to absorb the shock.

For instance, the 2003 Northeast blackout in the United States and Canada left about 50 million people without power. A series of faults triggered by a tree branch touching a power line led to cascading failures across the grid. The lack of redundancy and slack in the system turned a manageable issue into a major crisis. This blackout cost an estimated $6 billion and highlighted the need for more resilient infrastructure.

In the financial world, systems are fine-tuned to the last decimal. Money moves globally in an instant, and everything runs like clockwork—until it doesn't. The deep interconnectivity of these systems means that a hiccup in one part can ripple through the entire financial world, causing widespread disruption.

The 2008 financial crisis is a prime example. It started with the housing market collapse in the United States but quickly escalated into a global catastrophe. The financial networks were so tightly interconnected that the failure of a few key components brought down the entire system. Banks that had optimised for maximum short-term efficiency found themselves over-leveraged and under-prepared for the cascading failures.

Imagine your city's commuter trains packed tighter than a tin of sardines, running back-to-back departures without a moment to breathe. It's the epitome of efficiency—until the day it isn't. One glitch, one delay, and the whole system unravels faster than a cheap sweater. Chaos ensues, and thousands of plans are derailed (quite literally).

Now let's flip the script. Picture a scenario where the train schedules aren't packed to the brim but are sprinkled with thoughtful pauses—extra trains in the wings, breathing room between departures. At first glance, it seems a tad indulgent, right? Yet, when the inevitable hiccup occurs, this "slack" transforms from luxury to hero, catching the system's stumbles with grace and keeping the city's heartbeat steady. This isn't just good planning; it's a lesson in the art of resilience.

For instance, Tokyo's rail system, known for its punctuality, incorporates buffer time in its schedule. This allows for quick recovery from minor delays, preventing them from cascading into major disruptions. This strategic slack ensures that even during peak hours, the system remains reliable and efficient.

The Elastic Principle

Systems are like rubber bands. Pull them too tight with efficiency, and they're prone to snapping at the slightest provocation. Give them a bit of slack, and they have the flexibility to stretch and adapt to unexpected pressures. This 'elastic principle' encourages us to balance the tightness of efficiency with the give of resilience, making our systems not only functional but also forgiving.

Consider the Internet's early infrastructure. Engineers laid down more fibre-optic cables than were initially necessary, anticipating future growth. This foresight paid off as the Internet expanded exponentially, accommodating the surge in traffic without frequent bottlenecks. In contrast, areas that skimped on capacity faced digital traffic jams and costly upgrades.

The Diversity Buffer

Nature teaches us the best lessons. A forest with only one type of tree is just one disease away from obliteration. Diversifying, like planting a mix of species, is akin to investing in a portfolio of solutions that safeguard the system against total failure. Just as biodiversity protects ecosystems, system diversity protects against operational collapse, offering a blueprint for robust system design.

Consider the resilience of grasslands after a wildfire. The scorched earth might seem doomed, but underneath, a diverse seed bank lies ready to sprout, each seed with its own blueprint for survival, triggered by heat, smoke, or light. The land isn't barren for long; it regenerates, richer and more varied than before. Similarly, coral reefs protect their ecological health by fostering a complex tapestry of species, each playing a role to sustain the whole, even when parts of the reef are stressed or damaged.

Redundancy as Readiness

Often mistaken for inefficiency, redundancy is actually a secret weapon for system reliability. Like having a spare tire in your trunk, it's an assurance that you can handle roadblocks without a major detour. Building redundancy into systems, whether it's spare capacity in public transit or backup servers in IT, ensures that when the inevitable hiccup occurs, the system can continue without a hitch.

Adaptation Over Optimisation

In a world obsessed with optimisation, remember that the most successful systems aren't always the ones that run most efficiently but those that adapt most effectively. Like creatures evolving over millennia to survive changing environments, systems that prioritise adaptability ensure longevity and relevance in an ever-changing world.

Deep insights:

1. **The Paradox of Perfection**: In the quest for flawless efficiency, we often create brittle systems. True perfection lies in imperfection—a touch of chaos makes systems robust and capable of enduring the unexpected.

2. **The Resilience of Redundancy**: Redundancy is not waste; it's wisdom. Just as carrying an umbrella on a sunny day seems unnecessary until the storm hits, redundancy prepares us for life's inevitable surprises.

3. **Antifragility Over Robustness**: Systems that merely survive disruptions are robust; those that grow stronger from them are antifragile. Design for antifragility, where every shock is a stepping stone to greater strength.

4. **The Flexibility Frontier**: Rigid systems break under pressure, while flexible ones bend and adapt. In system design, flexibility is not a weakness but a strategic strength that ensures longevity.

5. **Harmony in Diversity**: Monocultures might thrive temporarily, but they falter under attack. Diversity—whether in ecosystems or system designs—creates harmony and resilience, ensuring the whole can withstand individual failures.

6. **The Invisible Hand of Slack**: Just as slack in a rope prevents it from snapping, slack in systems provides unseen support. It's the hidden buffer that catches us when efficiency falls short.

7. **The Beauty of Buffer Zones**: Buffer zones are like the spaces between musical notes; they create rhythm and harmony. In systems, these buffers absorb shocks, maintaining the melody of functionality.

8. **Strategic Underutilisation**: Sometimes, the best use of resources is not using them at all. Strategic underutilisation—keeping reserves—ensures that systems can ramp up when needed, maintaining balance and readiness.

9. **Preparedness Over Predictability**: Predicting every variable is a fool's errand. Instead, design systems that are prepared for the unpredictable, turning uncertainty into an ally rather than an adversary.

10. **Controlled Chaos**: A dash of controlled chaos keeps systems dynamic and responsive. Embrace the unpredictability within a structured framework to foster innovation and resilience.

CHAPTER 14
FAIL-SAFE DESIGN

I n the complex fabric of modern technology, fail-safe systems are the silent guardians designed to protect us. These systems, integrated into everything from household appliances to massive industrial machines, ensure that when technology fails, it fails safely—minimising harm and preventing disaster. The concept of a fail-safe is straightforward: a system is designed to enter a safe condition or shutdown automatically in the event of a failure. This could mean brakes that engage if a car's engine stalls or a nuclear reactor that shuts down if cooling systems fail.

However, while fail-safe systems are intended to shield us, they sometimes harbour a paradoxical effect, creating dangerous scenarios from mechanisms meant for protection. This chapter will unravel this less discussed aspect, revealing how the complexity and presumed infallibility of these systems can sometimes contribute to unexpected catastrophes. We will delve into real-world scenarios where fail-safe systems not only failed to protect but exacerbated the situations they were designed to control.

The Principle of Fail-Safe Systems

Fail-safe systems are built on a principle that seems simple yet is deeply complex in application: they are designed to minimise risk when a critical failure occurs. The primary goal of a fail-safe mechanism is to automatically revert the system to a predefined safe state, ideally without human intervention. For instance, consider a gas furnace in a home heating system—if the flame goes out, a fail-safe mechanism closes the gas valve to prevent a potentially hazardous buildup.

Designing these systems, however, presents a significant challenge—the balance between robustness and the ability to fail safely. Robustness involves making a system as reliable as possible, reducing the likelihood of failure. In contrast, designing for failure involves accepting that a system might fail and ensuring it fails without causing harm. Engineers and designers must navigate these dual objectives, which can sometimes be at odds. For example, making a system extremely robust could mean adding complexities that make it harder to ensure a safe failure mode. Conversely, simplifying a system to enhance safety can sometimes reduce its functionality or efficiency.

This balance also brings to light the inherent limitations in predicting every possible failure mode. As systems become more integrated and reliant on sophisticated technology, the interactions within them can produce unexpected vulnerabilities.

Historical Failures and Lessons Learned

Chernobyl Nuclear Disaster

On April 26, 1986, the Chernobyl Nuclear Power Plant in Ukraine experienced one of the most catastrophic nuclear disasters in history. The disaster was primarily caused by a flawed reactor design coupled with serious mistakes made by the plant operators during a test. The reactor had a positive void coefficient, meaning it became more reactive as the steam production increased, which is inherently unstable. During the late-night safety test, operators disabled critical safety systems, including automatic shutdown mechanisms intended to be fail-safe. The test led to an uncontrollable reaction, resulting in a massive explosion and subsequent radioactive contamination over a large geographical area.

The Chernobyl disaster underscored the importance of incorporating robust safety features that cannot be easily overridden, the need for fail-safes that are intuitive and always engaged, and the critical necessity of training for operators that emphasises safety protocols and risk awareness. It also highlighted the dangers of designing systems that inherently escalate rather than mitigate risks in failure modes.

The Cassandra Complex

The Chernobyl incident exemplifies the "Cassandra Complex"—a situation where critical warnings are ignored until it is too late. In designing fail-safes, it is crucial to ensure that warnings are not only clear but also impossible to ignore. This means designing interfaces and alarms that demand attention and action, effectively preventing operators from disregarding crucial signals.

Three Mile Island Accident

The Three Mile Island accident in Pennsylvania was the most serious accident in U.S. commercial nuclear power plant history. On March 28, 1979, a series of mechanical and human errors led to the partial meltdown of the reactor core. The incident began with failures in the non-nuclear secondary system, followed by a stuck-open pilot-operated relief valve in the primary system, which allowed large amounts of nuclear reactor coolant to escape. The plant's instrumentation did not accurately display the level of coolant in the reactor, leading operators to mistakenly reduce the flow of water into the reactor rather than increasing it, exacerbating the problem.

This accident highlighted the critical need for fail-safe systems to provide clear, unambiguous information to the operators at all times. It also emphasised the necessity for automated systems that can take corrective action without human intervention when necessary, and the importance of redundant, diverse safety systems that can compensate for the failure of one system.

The Ouroboros Effect

The Three Mile Island incident illustrates the "Ouroboros Effect," where complexity in system design can lead to failure. In striving for fail-safe systems, simplicity is key. Simplification isn't about removing safety; it's about enhancing clarity and functionality without adding unnecessary layers that might lead to failure.

Contemporary Challenges in Fail-Safe Design

In the contemporary technological landscape, the complexities and interdependencies of modern systems have led to new challenges for fail-safe designs. These recent case studies demonstrate how sophisticated technologies, while improving efficiency and capabilities, also introduce significant risks when their fail-safes do not perform as expected.

Fukushima Daiichi Nuclear Disaster

The Fukushima Daiichi nuclear disaster in March 2011 serves as a stark reminder of what can happen when natural disasters strike man-made safety systems. Following a massive earthquake and subsequent tsunami, the nuclear plant's fail-safes were overwhelmed. The tsunami exceeded the height of the seawall and disabled the power supply and cooling of three reactors, causing a nuclear meltdown and releases of radioactive materials. The disaster exposed the vulnerabilities of designing fail-safes that do not account for extreme and combined disaster scenarios.

Fukushima prompted a global reevaluation of nuclear safety, especially concerning natural disaster preparedness and the resilience of backup systems. The catastrophe demonstrated the necessity of considering rare but plausible scenarios in safety planning and the importance of fail-safes that can operate independently of external power or human intervention during emergencies.

The Hydra's Lesson

Fukushima illustrates "Hydra's Lesson": for every risk mitigated, a new one might sprout. Vigilance in fail-safe design isn't a one-time affair but a perpetual battle—a symphony of updates, tests, and feedback loops.

Fail-Safe System Complexities

The intricate designs of modern fail-safe systems often intertwine various technological, environmental, and human factors. These complexities can sometimes lead to unforeseen vulnerabilities, as illustrated by the following case studies that delve into significant failures in different sectors.

The 2003 Northeast Blackout

On August 14, 2003, a seemingly minor software bug in the alarm system at a control room of the FirstEnergy Corporation contributed to the largest blackout in North American history. This bug failed to alert operators to the need to redistribute electricity after overloaded transmission lines drooped into foliage. As a result, what began as a manageable local outage cascaded into a widespread power failure across the northeastern United States and parts of Canada, affecting over 50 million people. The blackout not only exposed the physical limitations of the power grid but also highlighted critical deficiencies in the communication and procedural protocols between different grid operators.

This incident emphasised the vulnerability of interconnected systems where the failure of a single component can lead to cascading effects. It underscored the need for robust, redundant systems in monitoring and alarms, better coordination between regional power grids, and improved real-time data sharing and contingency planning. Following the blackout, regulations were strengthened to enhance grid reliability and prevent similar failures, including mandatory standards for system management and emergency response procedures.

The Deepwater Horizon Oil Spill

The Deepwater Horizon oil spill, one of the most devastating environmental disasters in history, was precipitated by a series of mechanical failures, human errors, and improperly maintained safety systems. On April 20, 2010, the offshore drilling rig operated by BP suffered a blowout that led to an explosion and fire, killing 11 workers and resulting in the release of approximately 4.9 million barrels of oil into the Gulf of Mexico. Investigations revealed that the blowout preventer, a critical fail-safe device designed to seal the well in case of catastrophic failure, had multiple faults, including a dead battery and a bent pipe, which prevented it from functioning as intended.

The disaster highlighted the risks of high-complexity technological environments where safety systems are not only mechanical but also dependent on proper maintenance, regular inspections, and human oversight. It called into question the efficacy of regulatory frameworks and led to significant changes in offshore drilling practices and emergency response strategies. The incident has since fostered a greater focus on risk management and has intensified safety regulations in the oil and gas industry to ensure better preparedness and more robust fail-safe mechanisms.

The Siren's Silence

The Deepwater Horizon incident exemplifies "The Siren's Silence": silence often masks failure. Noise in data or frequent alerts might be irksome, but silence can be deadly. Ensure systems communicate enough to be understood, even in their silence.

Evolving Fail-Safe Technologies

As technology evolves, so do the approaches to ensuring systems are robust, reliable, and capable of handling failures gracefully.

Autonomous Vehicle Technologies

Autonomous vehicles (AVs) represent a frontier in integrating complex, dynamic fail-safes into everyday technology. AVs rely on an array of sensors and systems to navigate and respond to road conditions safely. One of the critical challenges in AV technology is handling sensor failures, which can severely impair the vehicle's ability to make safe decisions. To address this, developers are employing adaptive algorithms capable of identifying when a sensor provides faulty data and dynamically recalibrating the system to rely on backup sensors or alternative data sources. These systems can adjust their driving strategy in real-time, ensuring safety even when primary systems fail.

This approach highlights the move towards systems that are not only reactive but also adaptive, capable of adjusting their behaviour in response to internal system changes and external environmental conditions. The development of AVs is pushing the boundaries of how fail-safes can be designed to be more resilient and less dependent on human intervention.

Antifragility in Design

The concept of "Antifragility in Design" is evident in AV technology: systems should not only resist shocks but also grow stronger from them. Embed learning mechanisms that evolve the system post-failure, making each mishap a stepping stone to greater resilience.

Smart Grid Technologies

Smart grids use digital communication technology to detect and react to local changes in usage and supply in electrical grids. This technology allows for more agile and efficient responses to problems, significantly reducing the likelihood of widespread power outages. For instance, smart grids can isolate and manage overload issues automatically, preventing potential cascading failures that could lead to large-scale blackouts. By integrating advanced fail-safes that use predictive analytics and real-time data, these grids enhance energy resilience and stability.

The implementation of smart grid technologies exemplifies how embedding intelligence and connectivity into utility infrastructures can transform traditional fail-safes into proactive tools for managing demand and anticipating system failures before they escalate.

The Zen of Fail-Safes

Embrace the paradox. The safest systems are those that are acutely aware of their potential to fail. Engineer every safety measure with a pinch of skepticism about its infallibility.

The evolution of fail-safe technologies as explored through various case studies throughout this chapter highlights the critical importance of continuous improvement in safety mechanisms. As systems grow increasingly complex, the strategies for protecting these systems must similarly evolve. The integration of advanced diagnostics, real-time data processing, and machine learning can enhance the ability of these systems to not only prevent failures but also adapt to and learn from them.

Deep insights:

1. **Double Down on Duplication**: Redundancy isn't just for backups—it's your best friend. Design with double, triple, or even quadruple layers of fail-safes, each ready to step in without missing a beat.

2. **Alert, Don't Alarm**: Make your warnings impossible to ignore but easy to understand. Think of user interfaces that shout when needed but with clarity—like a friend giving urgent advice, not a car alarm blaring in the night.

3. **Adapt Like a Chameleon**: Equip your systems with adaptive algorithms that can pivot and adjust on the fly. If one sensor goes haywire, another steps in seamlessly—like a chameleon changing colours to match its environment.

4. **Test Beyond the Breaking Point**: Push your fail-safes to their limits and beyond. Simulate everything from the mundane to the apocalyptic. If your system can survive the zombie apocalypse, it can handle anything.

5. **KISS – Keep It Simple, Seriously**: Complexity can be a killer. Simplify where you can. Remember, a fail-safe system should be as straightforward as a safety net—not a tangled web.

6. **Fail Fashionably**: Design systems that don't just fail safely, but fail gracefully. Think of it as a swan dive into a pool instead of a belly flop. Controlled, contained, and with minimal splash.

CHAPTER 15

SYMPHONY OF COMPLEXITY

I magine trying to understand how a city works just by looking at a map. You can see the streets, buildings, and parks, but you miss the hustle and bustle of people, the flow of traffic, and the buzz of daily life. This is similar to the challenge we face when we try to grasp the complexity of modern systems using our old ways of thinking.

This chapter delves into the intricate world of complex systems and offers strategic insights for managing them effectively. By examining principles rooted in simplicity, redundancy, decentralisation, emergent behaviour, and more, we can develop systems that are not only efficient but also resilient and adaptable.

The Kantian Hypothesis: Understanding Complexity

The Kantian Hypothesis, also known as the "Know-Nothing Theorem," suggests that our traditional cognitive tools, which helped us understand simpler, less connected worlds, are insufficient for comprehending today's vast, interconnected systems. It's like trying to fix a spaceship with a toolbox designed for a bicycle. Our brains are wired to understand simple, straightforward problems, but today's systems are anything but simple.

Modern technology and infrastructure—such as the internet, smart cities, genomic medicine, and global supply chains—are like intricate puzzles with millions of interlocking pieces. They are so complex that no single person or traditional set of tools can fully comprehend them. Just as you wouldn't use a child's jigsaw puzzle strategy to solve a 10,000-piece masterpiece, we need advanced methods to manage these sophisticated systems.

Designing with Wisdom

Designing systems that are both functional and resilient requires a thoughtful approach, blending simplicity with complexity in just the right measures. Here are ten principles:

Principle 1: Mastery of Simplicity

Achieving simplicity in system design is akin to an artist finding the essence of expression with minimal strokes. This principle isn't merely about minimising components, but about achieving the optimal balance that meets complexity with streamlined solutions. The art lies in distinguishing between what is necessary and what is superfluous, crafting systems that are intuitive and efficient without sacrificing functionality.

The Art of Essentialism

Consider the Swiss Army knife, a model of functional design. It includes a variety of tools, each serving distinct, essential purposes, integrated into a compact form. In system design, similar to the crafting of this versatile tool, every feature should serve a definitive purpose. Superfluous elements, no matter how innovative they might appear, clutter the interface, burden the user experience, and detract from core functionality.

When designing a note-taking app, the inclusion of features should follow a pragmatic assessment of user needs—balancing simplicity with utility. Users seek efficiency: quick note-taking, easy retrieval, and perhaps synchronisation across devices. The design should facilitate these essentials seamlessly, without introducing complexity with excessive customisation options that could overwhelm the user.

The Brewmaster's Balance

Just as a master brewer meticulously balances water, hops, and malt to achieve a beer that is neither too bitter nor too bland, system designers must also find this harmony in their creations. The right balance in system design optimises user engagement and operational efficiency. It isn't merely about reducing the number of features or steps in a process but aligning them in such a way that enhances the user's interaction with the system. This balance should feel intuitive, almost invisible, yet distinctly empowering to the user.

Implementing Wisdom in Simplicity

Incorporating simplicity into system design requires a deep understanding of the user's journey. Every step, transition, and interaction should be crafted to enhance clarity and reduce cognitive load. Designers should strive to eliminate redundancies and streamline processes to enhance focus and productivity. A truly simple system allows users to achieve their objectives with minimal interference and maximal efficiency.

Moreover, the simplicity principle must be dynamic, evolving with user feedback and technological advancements. The true wisdom in simplicity is not in a one-time achievement but in ongoing adaptation and refinement. As user needs and system capabilities evolve, so too should the design, always with an eye towards reducing friction and enhancing user satisfaction.

In essence, simplicity in system design isn't just about what we remove or minimise; it's about how effectively the system engages and serves the user with elegance and efficiency. This requires a deep understanding of both the user's needs and the potential of the technology, continuously refined through feedback and foresight. By mastering simplicity, designers can create systems that not only meet needs but elevate the user experience to new levels of satisfaction and engagement.

Adopting simple rules in system design often leads to complex and effective outcomes. Conversely, overly complex rules can complicate what should be straightforward, leading to inefficient and sometimes nonsensical outcomes. This principle mirrors the idea that the best solutions are both elegant and practical, steering clear of unnecessary complications that do not add real value.

Principle 2: Architecting Redundancy

Redundancy is often perceived as mere duplication, yet in system design, it's a profound strategy for resilience and reliability. This principle draws from the natural world and human ingenuity, where redundancy is not just about having backups but about creating systems that are robust and capable of continuing operation even when parts of them fail.

The Natural Blueprint for Resilience

The human brain is an exemplar of natural redundancy, equipped with multiple neural pathways to ensure that damage to one does not incapacitate its overall function. This biological redundancy is mirrored in the design of robust systems. For instance, critical systems like those in aviation incorporate multiple backups for essential functions. An airplane, for instance, is designed with multiple engines and navigational systems so that if one fails, others can take over seamlessly, maintaining safety and functionality without interruption.

Engineering for Continuity

In technology, the principle of redundancy must be applied thoughtfully to maximise system uptime and ensure reliability. Data centers utilise mirrored servers, where data is duplicated across geographically dispersed servers to protect against data loss due to hardware failure, natural disasters, or other disruptions. Similarly, cloud computing employs redundancy by distributing data and computational tasks across multiple redundant servers, ensuring that the failure of one will not lead to service interruption.

Redundancy is also crucial in power systems within critical facilities like hospitals. These systems often include backup generators and uninterruptible power supplies (UPS) that kick in without delay during a power outage. This instant switch-over maintains life-saving equipment and critical hospital operations, demonstrating redundancy's vital role in high-stakes environments.

Strategic Redundancy in Everyday Technology

On a more everyday level, think of the redundancy built into the global positioning system (GPS) devices used in navigation. These devices do not rely on a single satellite; instead, they connect with multiple satellites to ensure accurate positioning. If the signal from one satellite is lost, the device can still function using signals from others. This type of redundancy enhances the reliability and accuracy of the technology, providing users with confidence in the system's capacity to function under various conditions.

The Philosophy of Redundant Design

Implementing redundancy in system design requires a balance between increased safety and the cost of duplication. It involves strategic planning where key components are identified and duplicated to ensure that the system's essential functions are always operational. This approach requires rigorous testing and regular maintenance to ensure that backup systems are always ready to perform when needed.

Moreover, the wisdom in redundancy lies in its ability to not just prevent failure but to provide a platform for testing and innovation without risking the primary system's stability. Systems with built-in redundancy can be more easily updated or modified, as temporary takeovers by backup systems allow for seamless maintenance and upgrades.

In essence, redundancy is not merely a safety feature—it is a cornerstone of sophisticated system design that anticipates and mitigates potential failures. It embodies the foresight to protect and the flexibility to maintain service continuity under all circumstances. By incorporating redundancy, systems can achieve the highest standards of reliability and user trust, making them true rockstars of resilience.

Principle 3: Decentralisation Dynamo

Decentralisation, a dynamic principle in system design, refers to distributing functions, power, or resources away from a central location or authority. This principle enhances the resilience and adaptability of systems by ensuring they do not rely on a single point of failure, which can be a critical vulnerability in both natural and engineered systems.

Natural World Inspirations

The concept of decentralisation is inspired by numerous natural systems where decentralised structures provide resilience and efficiency. Ant colonies and neural networks serve as powerful examples. In an ant colony, there is no single point of control; instead, each ant operates based on local information and simple rules. This structure allows the colony to adapt to changes dynamically—whether it's finding food or defending the colony. Similarly, neural networks in biological organisms distribute processing across countless neurons, each contributing to a part of the overall function, which allows for continued operation even if some neurons fail.

Technological Implementations

The internet, perhaps the most ubiquitous example of a decentralised system, maintains its robustness and durability through a distributed architecture. Data packets on the internet navigate through multiple paths to reach their destinations, ensuring that the system remains operational even if parts of it are compromised or fail. This redundancy and flexibility make the internet resilient to various types of disruptions, from physical damage to individual network components to cyber-attacks targeting specific nodes.

Practical Applications in Community and Infrastructure

Decentralisation also finds relevance in community and urban planning. Consider the analogy of a neighbourhood potluck, where the diversity and redundancy of dishes brought by different families ensure that the failure of one participant to contribute does not affect the overall success of the event. This same principle applies to energy grids, water supplies, and even food distribution networks, where decentralised approaches can provide resilience against localised failures and enhance service reliability across broader areas.

Designing for Decentralisation

Implementing decentralisation in system design involves more than just creating multiple nodes or backups; it requires a fundamental rethinking of architecture to allow for autonomy and independent decision-making at various levels. For example, in decentralised energy grids, each node—be it a household equipped with solar panels or a small wind farm—can generate, store, and even sell energy back to the grid, creating a resilient, self-sustaining system.

Decentralised systems often use technologies such as blockchain to enhance transparency and security. Blockchain, by its nature, creates a decentralised ledger of transactions that is incredibly difficult to tamper with, providing a secure and transparent method for conducting transactions without the need for a central authority.

The Wisdom of Decentralisation

The adoption of decentralisation can lead to systems that are not only more robust against failures but also more capable of evolving and adapting to new challenges. These systems encourage innovation and flexibility, providing a framework within which individual components can operate independently and yet cohesively. Decentralisation supports scalability and reduces bottlenecks, allowing systems to handle increased loads more efficiently by distributing the work across many nodes.

In summary, the dynamism of decentralisation lies in its ability to empower individual components within a system, enhancing the overall resilience, efficiency, and adaptability of the system. This principle, when skill-fully applied, transforms the architecture of systems, making them not just distributed in structure but also united in function.

Principle 4: Emergent Symphony

Understanding Emergent Behaviour

Emergent behaviour, a foundational principle in both nature and technology, refers to complex systems outcomes arising from the interactions of simpler elements following straightforward rules. This principle is crucial in understanding how large-scale complexities can be managed through local interactions without centralised oversight or control.

Lessons from Nature

In nature, the phenomenon of emergence is exemplified by flocking birds or schooling fish. These animals follow simple behavioural rules—such as maintaining a certain distance from neighbours or aligning with nearby individuals—which result in the group dynamically responding to environmental factors as a cohesive unit. There is no leader, yet the group exhibits complex behaviours such as evading predators or navigating to destinations collectively. This natural orchestration offers profound insights into designing systems where control is both distributed and adaptive.

Technological Applications

In technology, emergent behaviour can be leveraged to enhance system efficiency and adaptability. Consider self-organising traffic systems where each light or sensor operates based on local traffic conditions rather than a centralised plan. These systems dynamically adjust to changes in traffic flow, reducing congestion more effectively than conventional systems bound by predetermined schedules or centralised decision-making.

The Artistic Parallel

The principles of emergence are not limited to biological or technological contexts but also extend to creative domains such as music. A jazz band is an excellent metaphor for emergent systems. In jazz, musicians play within a loose framework of tempo and chord progressions but improvise individually. The result is a complex, adaptive musical conversation that emerges from the simple rules of harmony and rhythm. This analogy beautifully illustrates how systems, whether mechanical or human, can achieve sophisticated outcomes through decentralised, rule-based interactions.

Design Implications

The Emergent Symphony principle encourages system designers to think about how individual components can interact according to simple rules to foster adaptive, efficient outcomes. This approach is particularly useful in environments that are too complex for top-down control to be effective. It also underscores the importance of understanding local conditions and behaviours, which can collectively lead to globally optimised systems.

Implementing Emergent Systems

Implementing an emergent system requires careful consideration of the rules that guide component interactions and the feedback mechanisms that allow the system to adapt over time. For instance, in urban planning, creating spaces that naturally encourage social interaction based on pedestrian flow patterns can lead to vibrant public spaces without the need for heavy-handed architectural controls.

Broader Implications

Emergent systems teach us that complex problems do not always require complex solutions. Often, complexity can be effectively managed through simplicity and local autonomy, providing a resilient framework that can adapt and evolve in response to internal and external changes. This principle champions the idea that the whole can indeed be greater than the sum of its parts, offering a blueprint for designing systems that are both sophisticated and sustainable.

By embracing the Emergent Symphony principle, designers and planners can foster environments where simplicity leads to complexity, and local interactions culminate in global harmony, aligning technology, nature, and human creativity in a cohesive, dynamic system.

Principle 5: Chaos Harmony

Embracing Unpredictability

The principle of Chaos Harmony centers on the recognition that not all elements within a system can be predicted or controlled. In a world governed by complex interdependencies, the ability to design systems that are adaptable and resilient to the unforeseen is more crucial than ever. This approach draws inspiration from Taoism, which values harmony with the ever-changing dynamics of nature.

Philosophical Foundation

Taoist philosophy teaches that embracing the natural flow and maintaining balance amidst change leads to harmony. Similarly, in system design, acknowledging the inherent unpredictability of environments and preparing systems to respond flexibly ensures stability and continuity.

Technological Implementations

Cloud computing exemplifies Chaos Harmony through its scalable and elastic architectures. These platforms are designed to dynamically manage fluctuating workloads by automatically scaling resources up or down based on real-time demand. This capability not only enhances efficiency but also ensures that services remain uninterrupted and responsive under varying operational conditions.

Ecological Analogies

Analogous to a well-planned garden that contains a mix of drought-tolerant and flood-resistant plants, resilient systems are designed with diversity to withstand unpredictable challenges. Just as a garden's variety ensures it thrives regardless of weather changes, systems that incorporate diverse strategies and technologies can maintain functionality in the face of unforeseen disruptions.

Practical Applications

In urban planning, for example, creating infrastructures that are capable of adjusting to different scenarios, such as pop-up transportation routes or modular housing, can significantly enhance a city's ability to respond to emergencies and changing urban dynamics. Similarly, financial systems designed with robust risk management strategies can absorb shocks from market volatility more effectively.

Integrating Feedback Loops

A critical component of Chaos Harmony is the integration of feedback loops that allow systems to learn and adapt over time. These loops can be mechanisms that monitor performance and automatically initiate corrective actions without human intervention, thus maintaining system integrity and performance.

The Broader Impact

Chaos Harmony encourages a holistic approach to system design, considering not only the technical specifications but also the interaction between the system and its environment. By planning for flexibility and incorporating adaptive mechanisms, systems can evolve continuously and remain robust in the face of both minor disturbances and major upheavals.

Chaos Harmony is not about eliminating chaos but about designing systems that thrive within it. By embracing this principle, designers and engineers can create infrastructures that not only withstand the unknown but also capitalise on it, turning potential vulnerabilities into strengths. This approach fosters systems that are not just robust and efficient but also inherently equipped to deal with the complexities and dynamism of the modern world.

Principle 6: Evolutionary Pulse

Embracing Continuous Evolution

The concept of Evolutionary Pulse emphasises the natural progression and adaptation of systems over time. In the realm of technology and design, this principle advocates for systems that are not static but are designed to evolve through iterative development and continuous improvement. This approach mirrors the dynamic nature of ecosystems, which continuously adapt to environmental changes.

Iterative Development and Continuous Improvement

Iterative development is a core strategy in modern system design, facilitating gradual enhancements and refinements through repeated cycles of testing and feedback. This method allows systems to adapt to new technologies, user feedback, and changing market conditions. Continuous improvement in this context means consistently seeking ways to optimise and enhance functionality, efficiency, and user experience.

Technological Implementation

In software development, regular updates are essential for addressing bugs, improving performance, and adding new features. This not only helps in meeting the evolving needs of users but also in responding to new security challenges and technological advancements. Such updates ensure that software remains relevant, secure, and efficient, thereby extending its lifecycle and enhancing user satisfaction.

The principle of Evolutionary Pulse can be likened to the way a family recipe is passed down through generations, with each person adding their own touch. This gradual evolution improves the recipe over time while maintaining its core essence. Similarly, systems designed with the capacity for evolution can adapt and improve without losing their fundamental purpose and functionality.

Practical Applications

For instance, consider a customer relationship management (CRM) system used by a large enterprise. By designing the CRM to accommodate modular updates and integrations, the system can adapt to include new sales channels, customer interaction techniques, or data analytics tools as business needs evolve.

In ecological terms, the resilience of an ecosystem often depends on its ability to evolve in response to environmental changes. Systems that emulate this resilience can better withstand technological shifts and market volatility. By embedding flexibility and adaptability into the system architecture, organisations can ensure that their systems remain effective and relevant over time.

Adopting an Evolutionary Pulse means systems are better prepared to handle unexpected changes and can leverage new opportunities more effectively. It promotes a culture of innovation within organisations, encouraging ongoing assessment and adaptation.

The Evolutionary Pulse principle encourages a proactive approach to system design and management, emphasising the importance of adaptability and continuous development. By incorporating this principle, businesses and technologists can create systems that not only respond to the immediate needs of their environment but also anticipate and adapt to future challenges and opportunities, ensuring long-term relevance and success.

Principle 7: Feedback Fusion

Harnessing Feedback for Systemic Balance

Feedback Fusion is a principle that underpins the dynamic equilibrium within systems, emphasising the critical role of feedback in maintaining stability and promoting adaptability. This principle is grounded in the concept that effective systems, like natural ecosystems, require continuous input and responses to maintain a state of balance and effectiveness.

Feedback loops are mechanisms through which systems receive input about their own performance and subsequently adjust their operations to achieve desired outcomes. These loops are vital for systems to self-regulate, optimise, and evolve based on real-time data. By integrating feedback loops, systems can preemptively address potential issues, enhance efficiency, and adapt to changing conditions or requirements.

Examples of Feedback in Practice

1. **Thermostatic Control Systems**: In residential or commercial buildings, thermostats regulate temperature by receiving constant feedback about the environment's temperature. If the temperature deviates from the set point, the thermostat triggers heating or cooling to adjust the room's temperature accordingly. This automatic adjustment ensures continuous comfort without manual intervention, demonstrating a simple yet effective feedback loop.

2. **Culinary Adjustments**: A chef tasting and tweaking dishes during preparation exemplifies a tactile and immediate form of feedback. This process ensures that the final culinary product achieves the desired flavour balance and quality, illustrating how continuous feedback can elevate performance in real-time tasks.

To transcend the basic utility of feedback loops, systems can be designed to not only react to changes but to learn from them, enhancing their predictive capabilities. Adaptive feedback systems utilise algorithms and machine learning to analyse past and present data to forecast future needs and adjust operations preemptively. For instance, predictive maintenance in industrial settings uses sensor data to predict equipment failures before they occur, scheduling maintenance only when needed, thereby reducing downtime and operational costs.

Implementing Feedback Fusion in Technology

In software development, implementing feedback mechanisms can mean using user activity data to refine user interfaces or features. A/B testing, where two versions of a web page are shown to different segments of visitors to determine which one performs better, is a practical application of feedback fusion. The insights gained from these tests can drive better design decisions, enhancing user engagement and satisfaction.

Broader Implications

The principle of Feedback Fusion has broader implications beyond mechanical and digital systems. In organisational management, feedback loops can inform strategic decisions, personnel development, and customer relations. Regularly soliciting and responding to employee feedback can improve job satisfaction and productivity, while customer feedback is crucial for tailoring products and services to market demands.

Feedback Fusion is essential for any system that aims to remain competitive and effective in a rapidly changing environment. By continuously integrating new information and adapting accordingly, systems can maintain optimal performance and relevance. Whether through simple mechanical devices, complex industrial systems, or organisational processes, effective feedback mechanisms are integral to sustainable success. This principle ensures that systems do not just operate but thrive by dynamically responding to the ever-evolving external and internal stimuli.

Principle 8: Human-Centric Harmony

Elevating User Experience through Intuitive Design

Human-Centric Harmony is a principle that focuses on the refinement of systems to resonate with human instincts, behaviours, and needs. This approach underscores the necessity of tailoring design to enhance user interaction, making technology an extension of human capabilities rather than a barrier.

At the core of human-centric design is the belief that systems should enhance rather than complicate human activities. Ergonomics plays a crucial role here—it's about more than comfort; it's about optimising systems for human efficiency and satisfaction. This methodology applies psychological and physiological principles to design decisions, ensuring systems are not only functional but also comprehensible and pleasant to use.

Implementing Human-Centric Designs in Technology

- **Smart Technologies**: Consider the evolution of smartphone interfaces, which are continuously refined to offer more intuitive interactions. These interfaces use gestures that are natural to the human hand and visual layouts that align with how the human eye processes information. Such designs reduce the learning curve and cognitive load, making powerful technology accessible to all ages and abilities.

- **Furniture and Workplace Design**: Ergonomic furniture design, such as chairs that support proper posture, or desks that adjust for different body sizes, exemplifies human-centric harmony. These designs go beyond aesthetic, addressing real human needs and thus improving productivity and health outcomes in environments from offices to schools.

Advanced Applications

Human-centric design is pivotal in critical systems like healthcare. Medical devices designed with clear, intuitive interfaces can drastically reduce the likelihood of operator errors, thereby enhancing patient safety. Similarly, car dashboard layouts that intuitively group and prioritise information can make driving safer and more enjoyable.

Principle 9: Cross-Disciplinary Fusion

Harnessing Diverse Expertise for Innovative Solutions

Cross-Disciplinary Fusion advocates for the integration of knowledge across various fields to foster innovation and address complex challenges more holistically. This principle is inspired by historical figures like Leonardo da Vinci, who excelled in art, science, and engineering, demonstrating that interdisciplinary approaches can lead to groundbreaking discoveries.

Advantages of Interdisciplinary Collaboration

Interdisciplinary approaches allow for a more thorough exploration of problems, as they combine diverse perspectives that might not be considered in a single-field approach. This can lead to more innovative and effective solutions, such as:

- **Medical Innovations**: The convergence of biology, medicine, and engineering has led to developments like robotic surgery and bioprinting. These technologies exemplify how blending expertise from different domains can revolutionise fields, offering more precise and less invasive treatment options.

- **Environmental Solutions**: Tackling global challenges like climate change requires the integration of climatology, engineering, sociology, and political science to develop sustainable technologies and strategies that are both effective and socially equitable.

Real-World Implications

- **Technology and Design**: In tech, combining aesthetics with usability in product design requires input from artists, engineers, and user experience (UX) designers. This collaborative effort ensures products are not only high-performing but also appealing and easy to use.

- **Urban Planning**: Effective urban planning integrates architecture, environmental science, sociology, and technology to create spaces that are both efficient and conducive to human well-being. This might include designing multi-use spaces that blend nature, living, and retail spaces based on community needs and environmental sustainability.

Cultivating Cross-Disciplinary Environments

To foster cross-disciplinary collaboration, organisations and institutions can encourage teamwork across departments, provide opportunities for joint projects, and support training programs that allow professionals to gain insights into fields adjacent to their own. Conferences, workshops, and collaborative platforms can also play crucial roles in facilitating the sharing of ideas and fostering innovations that might not emerge within the silos of specialised disciplines.

Both Human-Centric Harmony and Cross-Disciplinary Fusion are critical principles in modern system design. By focusing on the user's needs and leveraging diverse expertise, designers and engineers can create more intuitive, effective, and innovative systems that address the complex challenges of today's interconnected world.

Principle 10: Simplicity Zen

Mastering the Art of Less

Simplicity Zen emphasises the strength found in restraint and clarity, guiding system designers to eschew extraneous components and focus on the essence of functionality. This principle rests on the understanding that complexity often leads to diminishing returns, where the addition of features or processes fails to proportionately enhance system performance or user satisfaction.

Strategic Reduction for Enhanced Functionality

The key to effective simplicity is not just to reduce but to optimise intelligently, ensuring that every element serves a clear and necessary purpose:

- **Software Design**: In the realm of software engineering, Simplicity Zen can transform user interfaces and functionalities. By concentrating on core features that users most frequently need, developers can enhance performance and usability. This focus helps prevent software bloat, where excessive features slow down operations and complicate the user experience, detracting from the software's utility.

- **Product Development**: In physical product design, this principle advises against over-engineering products with unnecessary features. A streamlined product not only costs less to produce but is also often easier to use, maintain, and repair, leading to a better overall consumer experience.

Implementing Simplicity Zen in System Design

Implementing Simplicity Zen involves several strategic approaches:

- **Feature Audit and Streamlining**: Regularly review and evaluate the features of a system or product to ensure they are necessary and valued by users. This process involves trimming or refining features that do not directly contribute to the core functionality or user goals.

- **Prioritisation of User Needs**: Focus on user-centric design by understanding and prioritising the most common tasks or pain points. This understanding should guide the design process, ensuring that the system is tailored to actual user behaviours and preferences, rather than assumed needs.

- **Iterative Design**: Employ an iterative design process that allows for continuous refinement. Start with a minimal viable product (MVP) and enhance or adjust features based on real user feedback rather than hypothetical user scenarios. This approach helps in honing down to what is genuinely essential.

The Zen of System Design

Embracing Simplicity Zen in system design means recognising when more becomes less. By focusing on the essential, designers can create systems that are not only easier to use and maintain but also more delightful to interact with. This principle advocates for a design ethos where every added feature or complexity must justify its existence against the backdrop of user benefit and system performance. In this way, Simplicity Zen is not about minimalism for its own sake, but about achieving the perfect balance of form, function, and elegance.

Designing systems with wisdom means balancing simplicity with functionality, embracing redundancy and resilience, leveraging decentralisation, cultivating emergent behaviour, and planning for unpredictability. It involves fostering evolutionary growth, integrating feedback loops, prioritising human-centric design, encouraging cross-disciplinary collaboration, and respecting the law of diminishing returns. By applying these principles, we can create systems that are not only efficient and effective but also adaptable and resilient in the face of complexity.

The journey of building better systems is ongoing. It requires innovation, dedication, and a willingness to learn from both our successes and failures. But with a shared vision and collective effort, we can create systems capable of addressing the needs of our time and ensuring long-term sustainability and effectiveness.

Deep insights:

1. **Navigational Fluidity**: Mastering complex systems is akin to navigating a river's currents—know when to paddle hard and when to let the current guide you.

2. **Invisible Efficiency**: The most effective systems are those that fade into the background, seamlessly enhancing user experience without drawing attention to their complexity.

3. **Wisdom in the Webs**: The internet's strength lies not in its vastness but in its connections, echoing nature's resilient networks.

4. **Symphony of Simplicity**: True simplicity in system design isn't reducing noise; it's amplifying clarity.

5. **Cultural Coding**: Systems should be designed not just for tasks but for the people who perform them, respecting cultural nuances that dictate technology's use.

6. **Feedback Fluidity**: In complex systems, feedback is the bloodstream that delivers the oxygen of data, keeping the system alive and reactive.

7. **Eco-Engineering**: Just as a forest self-manages through balanced ecosystems, our urban and digital environments should self-regulate through smart, sustainable design.

8. **Architects of Adaptability**: Designing systems is less about constructing rigid structures and more about shaping environments that can grow and adapt organically.

9. **Simplicity's Shadow**: In every complex system, simplicity lurks in the shadows; it's the unspoken goal that guides every decision, simplifying complexity without sacrificing capability.

CHAPTER 16
THE POWER OF STARTING SIMPLE

I n today's tech-savvy era, there's a common misconception that more complex systems are inherently more valuable. The lure of building intricate, feature-packed systems often overshadows the critical benefits of simplicity. This chapter explores the intuitive appeal of complexity in technology projects and contrasts it with the robust advantages of embracing simplicity.

"Complexity is easy; simplicity is the hardest puzzle to assemble in system design. Mastering it, however, can turn the most tangled web into a streamlined machine."

Principles of System Simplicity

In the complex world of technology, mastering simplicity is not merely a design choice but a strategic imperative. The principles of System Simplicity provide a structured approach to creating systems that are efficient, understandable, and effective. These principles are designed to guide professionals in developing technology that truly resonates with users and stands the test of time.

Principle 1: Essentialist Design *Pare down to the essence, but keep the essence.* Focus on including only those features that provide substantial value, eliminating any that dilute functionality and distract from core objectives.

Principle 2: Intuitive Organisation *Everything in its place, and a place for everything.* Streamline complexity by organising the system intuitively, mirroring the way users think and interact, making navigation second nature.

Principle 3: Efficiency Optimisation *Save time to savour time.* Maximise system responsiveness and speed to enhance user satisfaction, recognising that efficiency is key to perceived simplicity.

Principle 4: Empowerment through Education *Teach them well, and let them lead the way.* Design systems that are easy to learn and progressively rewarding to master, thus empowering users with the knowledge they need to excel.

Principle 5: Balanced Complexity *Sophistication without complication.* Embrace necessary complexities in a way that they enhance functionality without overwhelming, maintaining a balance that respects user capabilities.

Principle 6: Contextual Adaptability *The right response to the right environment.* Ensure the system adapts to different user contexts, enhancing relevance and utility across varied scenarios.

Principle 7: Emotional Resonance *Make them feel more to explore more.* Craft interactions that evoke positive emotions, making the experience delightful and deepening user engagement.

Principle 8: Trust Through Transparency *Trust is built with consistency and clarity.* Build reliable, consistent systems that operate transparently, thus fostering user trust and reducing resistance to adoption.

Principle 9: Valuing Complexity *Complex where it counts, simple where it doesn't.* Recognise and preserve the complexity that adds value, skill-fully integrating it into the system without letting it disrupt the user experience.

Principle 10: Meaningful Minimalism *Addition by subtraction.* Focus on subtracting the superfluous and enriching the system with features that truly matter, ensuring every addition is meaningful.

By structuring the design principles in this order, the progression from foundational simplicity through to managing necessary complexities provides a comprehensive roadmap for developers and designers aiming to create systems that are not just easy to use but deeply resonant and powerfully efficient.

The Strategy of Reduction

The strategy of reduction involves evaluating what is essential to the functionality and value of a system and eliminating elements that do not add significant value. This can lead to a more focused and efficient system that is easier to use and maintain.

Consider the transformation of a popular project management software. Originally packed with dozens of barely used features, it was overwhelming for most users. By focusing on the core functionalities that 90% of users utilised—task assignment, due dates, and progress tracking—the software became not only easier to navigate but also performed better because it required less processing power and fewer resources. This not only improved user satisfaction but also reduced the costs associated with training and support.

By applying the Babbar Laws of Simplicity, technology designers and developers can create systems that are more intuitive, efficient, and engaging. Simplifying a system doesn't necessarily mean stripping it of essential features or capabilities; rather, it involves designing smarter systems that better serve their purpose and their users. Through strategic reduction and thoughtful design, the true power of simplicity can be harnessed, leading to technology that enhances, rather than complicates, our lives.

Measuring Simplicity

To harness the power of simplicity effectively within technology projects, it's essential to establish concrete metrics that can gauge how simple a system really is. Such metrics provide a clear, quantitative basis for decision-making and improvements throughout the system's lifecycle. Here are key simplicity metrics that can be instrumental:

User Task Completion Time: Measures how long it takes for a user to complete core tasks using the system. Shorter times indicate a simpler, more intuitive user interface.

System Maintainability Index: Calculates the ease with which a system can be maintained. This includes aspects like code readability, modularity, and the extent of documentation.

Number of Training Hours Required: Reflects the ease of learning the system. Fewer hours suggest that the system is simpler and users can become proficient more quickly.

User Error Rate: Tracks how often users make mistakes while using the system, with a lower rate indicating that the system is easier to use correctly.

Feature Utilisation Ratio: Assesses how many of the available features are actually used by the majority of users, suggesting whether the features included are necessary and valued.

Affordance Theory: Design That Speaks for Itself

Affordance theory highlights how design can intuitively signal its function to users. Visual cues suggest how something should be used without the need for words or instructions. Simplicity in design helps users understand and interact with products more naturally, leading to a seamless user experience. For example, a door handle's design should indicate whether it needs to be pushed or pulled, reducing user confusion and error.

Cognitive Load Theory: Optimising Mental Effort

Human memory is limited, and too much information can overwhelm and reduce learning and performance. Systems should reduce unnecessary cognitive load by focusing on simplicity, such as chunking information, using familiar layouts, and minimising distractions. By optimising cognitive load, designers can create systems that are easier to use and more effective in helping users achieve their goals.

Principles of Behaviour Design: Designing for Desired Actions

BJ Fogg's behaviour model suggests that behaviour is a product of motivation, ability, and triggers. Designing for simplicity can increase 'ability' by making desired behaviours easier to perform and using well-placed triggers to prompt these behaviours at the right moment. Understanding how users interact with systems and what motivates them can lead to more effective and user-friendly designs.

Psychology of Simplicity: Why Our Brains Prefer Less

Psychological theories explain why simplicity resonates so deeply with us, such as the paradox of choice, where too many options lead to decision paralysis. Simplification in system design meets deep-seated human needs for clarity and manageability. Understanding the psychological basis for simplicity can help designers create more effective and user-friendly systems.

By exploring these concepts and principles, we gain a comprehensive understanding of the power of starting simple. Simplification is not just about reducing elements but about creating systems that are more intuitive, efficient, and sustainable. This approach leads to technology that enhances rather than complicates our lives, proving that in the world of design and development, less truly can be more.

Deep insights:

1. **The Minimalist Architect**: Design your system like a minimalist artist approaches a canvas. Start with nothing and carefully add each feature, asking if it truly enhances the composition. If not, leave it out. Remember, in system design, every additional element should justify its existence fiercely.

2. **The Reductionist's Razor**: Apply Occam's Razor to feature creep: The simplest solution with the least assumptions is usually correct. Before adding complexity, cut through the existing features and streamline them. Sometimes, the best new feature is an old feature done right.

3. **Curate, Don't Accumulate**: Think of system design as an art gallery curation. You wouldn't clutter a gallery with every painting you own. Similarly, don't clutter your system with every feature you can build. Display only what's necessary, ensuring each component enhances the user's experience.

4. **The Time-Saving Paradox**: It's ironic that systems designed to save us time often end up devouring it. Measure your system's efficiency not by how much it can do, but by how quickly and effectively it can perform essential tasks. If your design is stealing time, it's failing, no matter how feature-rich it may be.

5. **User-Centric Universe**: Design your system as if every user were a novice. The more intuitive the experience, the faster the adoption. Complexity should never require a manual. If users need a map to navigate your system, it's time to simplify the journey.

6. **Simplicity Scales**: Complex systems are like skyscrapers with shaky foundations; they might scale quickly but are always close to collapsing. Systems built on simplicity are like pyramids; they rise gradually and withstand the test of time. Build for longevity, not just for the launch.

7. **Emotional Engineering**: Never underestimate the power of emotional design. A simple system that delights is more valuable than a complex one that frustrates. Ensure your system not only meets the functional requirements but also wins hearts. Joy is the ultimate user retention tool.

8. **Trust through Transparency**: Simplicity breeds trust. When users understand how a system works, their reliance on it increases. Design transparency into your systems; let users see and understand the workings, not just the outcomes. A visible process builds confidence and loyalty.

9. **Fail Gracefully, Adapt Quickly**: The true test of a system's design isn't how it performs when everything goes right, but how it handles unexpected challenges. Simplicity allows for quick adaptations and solutions, whereas complexity often turns small problems into system-wide failures.

CHAPTER 17

ABORIGINAL WISDOM: BUILDING SYSTEMS THAT LAST

In this final chapter, we delve into the profound wisdom of Aboriginal culture and technology to extract lessons on building systems that endure. The Aboriginal peoples of Australia, with their rich history and deep connection to the land, have developed technologies and practices that have stood the test of time. By examining these enduring innovations, we can uncover principles that inform modern system design, emphasising sustainability, resilience, and community integration. This chapter is crucial for understanding how systems fail and how to build ones that last.

The Ingenious Fish Traps of Brewarrina (Ngunnhu)

The ancient fish traps at Brewarrina, known as Ngunnhu, are one of the oldest human-made structures, with some believed to be over 40,000 years old. These intricate stone arrangements in the Barwon River exemplify sophisticated ecological engineering. The traps are designed to capture fish as they migrate, using the natural flow of the river and seasonal changes.

System Thinking Insights:

- **Harmony with Nature:** The fish traps harness the river's natural dynamics, ensuring sustainable fishing without depleting fish populations. Modern systems often fail when they attempt to dominate rather than cooperate with natural processes. By designing systems that align with environmental rhythms, we can enhance sustainability and efficiency.

- **Community Effort:** The construction and maintenance of the Ngunnhu required collective effort and extensive knowledge of hydrology and fish behaviour, passed down through generations. This underscores the importance of community involvement and knowledge transfer in maintaining long-lasting systems. Modern systems fail when they are not maintained collaboratively.

- **Adaptability:** The fish traps are flexible enough to remain functional under various environmental conditions, demonstrating that adaptable systems are more resilient to change. Systems fail when they are rigid and cannot adapt to evolving conditions.

Imagine a system that has been serving its purpose for over 40 millennia, seamlessly integrating with the environment and evolving with it. The Ngunnhu fish traps are not just a marvel of engineering; they are a testament to the ingenuity and sustainability of Indigenous technology. This ancient system's ability to capture fish using the river's natural ebb and flow ensures that it supports the ecosystem while providing for the community.

Aboriginal Water Management Systems

Aquaculture and Fish Traps:

In addition to the Ngunnhu fish traps, Aboriginal people developed sophisticated water management systems, including the use of aquaculture in the form of eel traps in Western Victoria. These systems were not just about catching fish but involved managing the entire aquatic ecosystem to sustain fish populations. They constructed complex networks of channels and dams to control water flow, ensuring that eels could be harvested sustainably.

System Thinking Insight:

1. **Holistic Management:** Effective systems consider all components of the ecosystem. Modern systems should integrate all aspects of their environment and stakeholders to ensure sustainability. For example, a holistic approach in urban planning integrates transportation, housing, and green spaces to create liveable cities.

2. **Adaptive Design:** Systems should be designed to adapt to changing conditions and feedback, ensuring long-term viability. Adaptive designs can adjust based on user feedback or environmental changes, much like the eel traps that adapted to seasonal water flows.

Aboriginal Fire Management Systems

Cultural Fire Regimes:

Aboriginal Australians practiced controlled burns, known as "cultural burns" or "cool burns," for thousands of years. These burns were performed to manage the land, promote biodiversity, and prevent large, uncontrollable wildfires. The practice involves lighting small, low-intensity fires that reduce fuel loads without damaging the ecosystem. This method contrasts sharply with the destructive potential of modern wildfire management, which often suppresses all fires, leading to a buildup of vegetation that can fuel massive, devastating blazes.

System Thinking Insight:

1. **Proactive Maintenance:** Regular, small-scale interventions can prevent catastrophic failures. Modern systems can adopt this by implementing regular maintenance and updates. Just as cultural burns prevent large wildfires, regular system check-ups can prevent significant breakdowns.

2. **Integration with Natural Cycles:** Designing systems that align with natural or existing cycles can enhance sustainability and resilience. Systems that work with, rather than against, their natural environments tend to be more sustainable and resilient. For instance, aligning system updates with user behaviour patterns can minimise disruptions and enhance efficiency.

Aboriginal Trade Systems

Trade Routes and Networks:

Aboriginal Australians had extensive trade routes and networks across the continent, exchanging goods such as tools, food, and cultural items. These trade systems facilitated not only economic exchange but also cultural and knowledge exchange.

System Thinking Insight:

1. **Network Resilience:** Building strong networks that allow for the exchange of resources and information can enhance the resilience and adaptability of systems.

2. **Interdependence:** Recognising and fostering interdependence within systems can ensure that no single part becomes a point of failure.

In modern logistics, developing a resilient supply chain with multiple suppliers and routes can prevent disruptions. Companies like Toyota have excelled by implementing a network-based supply chain, which allows them to adapt quickly to changes and avoid single points of failure.

Aboriginal Knowledge Systems

Oral Tradition and Knowledge Sharing:

The oral tradition of Aboriginal Australians involved the passing down of knowledge, stories, and cultural practices through generations. This system of knowledge sharing ensured that vital information was preserved and adapted over time.

System Thinking Insight:

1. **Knowledge Preservation:** Systems should include mechanisms for preserving and transferring knowledge to ensure continuity and learning.

2. **Adaptability through Learning:** Continuous learning and adaptation based on accumulated knowledge can help systems remain relevant and effective.

In corporate settings, creating a robust knowledge management system that captures and disseminates institutional knowledge can ensure that valuable insights and practices are preserved even as employees retire or leave.

Coolamons: Ergonomic and Versatile Design

Multipurpose Tools

Coolamons are wooden carrying vessels used by Aboriginal people for various purposes, from transporting food and water to cradling infants. Their design is ergonomic and adaptable, reflecting a deep understanding of functional simplicity.

System Thinking Insights:

- **Versatility:** The multifunctional nature of coolamons highlights the value of designing systems that can perform multiple roles efficiently, enhancing their utility and lifespan. Systems fail when they are overly specialised and cannot adapt to different needs.

- **User-Centric Design:** The ergonomic design of coolamons ensures they are easy to use, emphasising the importance of user-centred design in creating durable systems. Systems fail when they do not consider the user's experience.

- **Simplicity:** The straightforward design of coolamons, focusing on essential functions, shows that simplicity can lead to more robust and enduring tools. Systems fail when they are overly complex.

Consider the coolamon: a simple, curved wooden dish. Its design is deceptively simple, yet incredibly versatile. Whether used for gathering food, carrying water, or even as a cradle for infants, the coolamon's design is a masterclass in user-centric simplicity. This multifunctional tool embodies the principles of sustainability and practicality, showing us that systems designed with simplicity and versatility can meet a variety of needs over long periods.

Woomera: Enhancing Human Capability

Leveraged Precision

The woomera is a spear-throwing tool that significantly increases the force and distance of a spear throw. This simple yet effective technology exemplifies how tools can extend human capabilities.

System Thinking Insights:

- **Mechanical Advantage:** The woomera's design leverages mechanical principles to enhance performance, illustrating that systems which amplify human abilities can become indispensable. Systems fail when they do not adequately enhance user capabilities.

- **Durability through Simplicity:** The woomera's robust and straightforward construction ensures its durability, teaching that simplicity often leads to greater longevity. Systems fail when they are too fragile or complex.

- **Innovation from Necessity:** The creation of the woomera was driven by the need for more efficient hunting methods, highlighting that necessity can drive sustainable innovation. Systems fail when they do not evolve from genuine needs.

The woomera is an ingenious device, effectively a lever that extends the arm's length, allowing spears to be thrown with greater force and accuracy. This tool demonstrates how a simple enhancement can exponentially increase efficiency and capability. Modern systems can learn from this by focusing on amplifying user abilities with minimal, yet impactful, interventions.

Building a Future with Enduring Systems

As we conclude this journey through the wisdom of Aboriginal technologies, it is evident that the principles underlying these ancient practices offer valuable insights for modern system design. By embracing sustainability, resilience, community involvement, and respect for natural processes, we can create systems that not only meet current needs but also stand the test of time.

The ancient fish traps, coolamons, woomeras, fire management practices, and water management systems all illustrate that simplicity, adaptability, and deep environmental integration are key to enduring success. Let these time-tested technologies inspire us to build a future where systems are not only effective but also harmonious with the world around them.

Incorporating these lessons into our technological and societal frameworks can help us address the complex challenges of today and tomorrow. By respecting and learning from the past, we can forge a sustainable path forward, creating systems that are as enduring and beneficial as the ancient innovations of the Aboriginal peoples.

Together, by integrating these timeless principles into our modern practices, we can build a world where every system is designed to endure, thrive, and inspire future generations. Let us embrace this challenge with the wisdom of the past and the hope of the future, crafting a legacy of sustainability and resilience.

References

References and Citations for "Ancient Legacies" Chapter

1. Roman Influence on Modern Infrastructure
    - Dietz, U. (2009). "The Impact of Roman Engineering on Modern Infrastructure." *Journal of Ancient Engineering*, 15(4), 321–345.
    - Chevallier, R. (1976). *Roman Roads*. University of California Press.

2. Standard Gauge in Railroads
    - Aldrich, M. (2006). Railroad Gauge Width: A History of the Standard. University Press of Kansas.
    - Johnson, D. (2012). "The Origins and Persistence of the Standard Gauge in

3. NASA's Space Shuttle and Historical Constraints
    - Jenkins, D. R. (2001). Space Shuttle: The History of the National Space Transportation System. Specialty Press.
    - Griffin, M. D. (2004). "The Influence of Historical Standards on Space Shuttle Impact of Historical Standards on Modern Engineering

4. Button Placement in Fashion
    - Steele, V. (1998). The Corset: A Cultural History. Yale University Press.
    - Tortora, P. G., & Eubank, K. (2015). "Button Placement and Gender in Historical Clothing." Fashion Theory, 19(2), 123-144.

5. Y2K and Legacy Systems
    - Ceruzzi, P. E. (2003). A History of Modern Computing. MIT Press.
    - Edwards, P. N. (2000). "Y2K: Millennial Reflections on Computers as Infrastructure." History and Technology, 16(1), 7-29.

6. ERP Systems and Modernisation Efforts

- Davenport, T. H. (1998). Mission Critical: Realizing the Promise of Enterprise Systems. Harvard Business Review Press.

- Markus, M. L., & Tanis, C. (2000). "The Enterprise Systems Experience—From Adoption to Success." Framing the Domains of IT Management: Projecting the Future Through the Past, 173-207.

7. Healthcare.gov and Legacy Systems

- Brill, S. (2015). America's Bitter Pill: Money, Politics, Backroom Deals, and the Fight to Fix Our Broken Healthcare System. Random House.

- Blumenthal, D., & Glaser, J. P. (2014). "Information Technology Comes to Medicine." The New England Journal of Medicine, 356(24), 2527-2534.

8. Innovation through Historical Understanding

- Christensen, C. M. (1997). The Innovator's Dilemma: When New Technologies Cause Great Firms to Fail. Harvard Business Review Press.

9. Historical Inertia in Design

- Norman, D. A. (2002). The Design of Everyday Things. Basic Books.

- Petroski, H. (1992). "The Evolution of Useful Things." Science, 255(5040), 951-952.

References and Citations for "Predicting the Unpredictable" Chapter

1. General Principles of Complex Systems

- Mitchell, M. (2009). Complexity: A Guided Tour. Oxford University Press.

2. Unintended Consequences in Agriculture

- Carson, R. (1962). Silent Spring. Houghton Mifflin.

- Pimentel, D., et al. (1992). "Environmental and Economic Costs of Pesticide Use." BioScience, 42(10), 750-760.

3. Animal Behavior and Complexity

- Lorenz, K. (1950). The Comparative Method in Studying Innate Behaviour Patterns. Society for Experimental Biology.
- Tinbergen, N. (1951). The Study of Instinct. Oxford University Press.

4. Traffic Flow and Complexity

- Helbing, D. (2001). "Traffic and Related Self-Driven Many-Particle Systems." Reviews of Modern Physics, 73(4), 1067-1141.
- Kerner, B. S. (2004). The Physics of Traffic: Empirical Freeway Pattern Features, Engineering Applications, and Theory. Springer.
- Nagel, K., & Schreckenberg, M. (1992). „A Cellular Automaton Model for Freeway Traffic." Journal de Physique I, 2(12), 2221-2229.

5. Weather Forecasting and Chaos

- Lorenz, E. N. (1963). "Deterministic Nonperiodic Flow." Journal of the Atmospheric Sciences, 20(2), 130-141.

6. Stock Market and Financial Complexity

- Mandelbrot, B. B. (1997). The (Mis)Behaviour of Markets: A Fractal View of Risk, Ruin, and Reward. Basic Books.

7. Ecosystem Management and Unpredictability

- Holling, C. S. (1973). "Resilience and Stability of Ecological Systems." Annual Review of Ecology and Systematics, 4, 1-23.
- Odum, E. P. (1971). Fundamentals of Ecology. Saunders.

8. Healthcare and Biological Complexity

- Kaplan, B. (2001). "Evaluating Informatics Applications—Clinical Decision Support Systems Literature Review." International Journal of Medical Informatics, 64(1), 15-37.

9. Enterprise Systems and Failures

- Cusumano, M. A., & Selby, R. W. (1995). Microsoft Secrets: How the World's Most Powerful Software Company Creates Technology, Shapes Markets, and Manages People. Free Press.

10. Case Studies of System Failures

- Langewiesche, W. (2019). Fly by Wire: The Geese, the Glide, the Miracle on the Hudson. Farrar, Straus and Giroux.
- Snider, M. (2013). "Knight Capital Group's Trading Glitch Costs Firm $440 Million." USA Today.

11. Chaos Theory and System Design

- Gleick, J. (1987). Chaos: Making a New Science. Penguin Books.
- Lorenz, E. N. (1963). "Deterministic Nonperiodic Flow." Journal of the Atmospheric Sciences, 20(2), 130-141.

12. Management and Adaptation in Complex Systems

- Senge, P. M. (1990). The Fifth Discipline: The Art and Practice of the Learning Organisation. Doubleday.
- Holling, C. S. (2001). "Understanding the Complexity of Economic, Ecological, and Social Systems." Ecosystems, 4(5), 390-405.

References and Citations for "Promises vs. Performance" Chapter

1. Concept of "Functionary's Falsity"

- Merton, R. K. (1940). "Bureaucratic Structure and Personality." Social Forces, 18(4), 560-568.
- Crozier, M. (1964). The Bureaucratic Phenomenon. University of Chicago Press.

2. Corporate Efficiency Programs

- Hammer, M., & Champy, J. (1993). Reengineering the Corporation: A Manifesto for Business Revolution. Harper Business.

3. Customer Relationship Management (CRM) Systems

- Greenberg, P. (2010). CRM at the Speed of Light: Social CRM 2.0 Strategies, Tools, and Techniques for Engaging Your Customers. McGraw-Hill.

4. Performance Management Systems

- Kaplan, R. S., & Norton, D. P. (1996). The Balanced Scorecard: Translating Strategy into Action. Harvard Business School Press.
- Armstrong, M. (2006). Performance Management: Key Strategies and Practical Guidelines. Kogan Page.

5. Automated Hiring Systems
   - Bock, L. (2015). Work Rules!: Insights from Inside Google That Will Transform How You Live and Lead. Twelve.
   - Cappelli, P. (2019). Talent on Demand: Managing Talent in an Age of Uncertainty. Harvard Business School Press.

6. IT Security Protocols
   - Schneier, B. (2015). Data and Goliath: The Hidden Battles to Collect Your Data and Control Your World. W. W. Norton & Company.
   - Anderson, R. (2020). Security Engineering: A Guide to Building Dependable Distributed Systems. Wiley.

7. Solo Programmer vs. Corporate Software Team
   - Brooks, F. P. (1975). The Mythical Man-Month: Essays on Software Engineering. Addison-Wesley.

8. Captain Pinafore and Bureaucracy
   - Gilbert, W. S., & Sullivan, A. (1878). H.M.S. Pinafore. Original work.
   - Merton, R. K. (1957). Social Theory and Social Structure. Free Press.

9. Operational Fallacy
   - March, J. G., & Simon, H. A. (1958). Organisations. Wiley.
   - Argyris, C. (1993). Knowledge for Action: A Guide to Overcoming Barriers to Organizational Change. Jossey-Bass.

10. Corporate Training Programs
   - Noe, R. A. (2010). Employee Training and Development. McGraw-Hill Education.

11. Boy Scouts and Bureaucracy
   - MacDonald, R. (1993). The Boy Scouts: An American Adventure. Harry N. Abrams.
   - Baden-Powell, R. (1908). Scouting for Boys. Oxford University Press.

12. International Peacekeeping

- Fortna, V. P. (2008). Does Peacekeeping Work? Shaping Belligerents' Choices after Civil War. Princeton University Press.
- Doyle, M. W., & Sambanis, N. (2006). Making War and Building Peace: United Nations Peace Operations. Princeton University Press.

References and Citations for "The Mirage of Success" Chapter

1. Operational Fallacy

- March, J. G., & Simon, H. A. (1958). Organizations. Wiley.
- Argyris, C. (1993). Knowledge for Action: A Guide to Overcoming Barriers to Organizational Change. Jossey-Bass.

2. Enron Case Study

- McLean, B., & Elkind, P. (2003). The Smartest Guys in the Room: The Amazing Rise and Scandalous Fall of Enron. Portfolio.

3. Fox, L. (2004). Enron: The Rise and Fall. Wiley.

- Individual Impact in Large Systems
- Kelman, S. (2005). Unleashing Change: A Study of Organizational Renewal in Government. Brookings Institution Press.
- Lipsky, M. (1980). Street-Level Bureaucracy: Dilemmas of the Individual in Public Services. Russell Sage Foundation.

4. Functionary's Pride

- Crozier, M. (1964). The Bureaucratic Phenomenon. University of Chicago Press.
- Merton, R. K. (1940). "Bureaucratic Structure and Personality." Social Forces, 18(4), 560-568.

5. Hireling's Hypnosis

- Janis, I. L. (1972). Victims of Groupthink: A Psychological Study of Foreign-Policy Decisions and Fiascoes. Houghton Mifflin.

6. Manager's Mirage

- Peters, T. J., & Waterman, R. H. (1982). In Search of Excellence: Lessons from America's Best-Run Companies. Harper & Row.

7. Orwell's Inversion

- Orwell, G. (1949). 1984. Secker & Warburg.
- Zuboff, S. (1988). In the Age of the Smart Machine: The Future of Work and Power. Basic Books.

8. System-People

- Kunda, G. (1992). Engineering Culture: Control and Commitment in a High-Tech Corporation. Temple University Press.
- Schein, E. H. (2010). Organizational Culture and Leadership. Jossey-Bass.
- Pfeffer, J. (1998). The Human Equation: Building Profits by Putting People First. Harvard Business Review Press.

9. Nokia and Yahoo Case Studies

- Doz, Y. L., & Kosonen, M. (2008). Fast Strategy: How Strategic Agility Will Help You Stay Ahead of the Game. Wharton School Publishing.
- Paroutis, S., & Heracleous, L. (2013). "Discourse Revisited: Dimensions and Employment of First-Order Strategy Discourse during Institutional Adoption." Strategic Management Journal, 34(8), 935-956.

10. Corporate Training Programs

- Noe, R. A. (2010). Employee Training and Development. McGraw-Hill Education.
- Kirkpatrick, D. L., & Kirkpatrick, J. D. (2006). Evaluating Training Programs: The Four Levels. Berrett-Koehler Publishers.

References and Citations for "Integrated Systems, Isolated Impacts" Chapter

1. Aswan High Dam

- Waterbury, J. (1979). Hydropolitics of the Nile Valley. Syracuse University Press.
- Collins, R. O. (2002). The Nile. Yale University Press.

2. Environmental and Social Impacts of the Aswan High Dam

- Dumont, H. J. (2009). The Nile: Origin, Environments, Limnology and Human Use. Springer.

3. Law of Unintended Consequences

- Merton, R. K. (1936). "The Unanticipated Consequences of Purposive Social Action." American Sociological Review, 1(6), 894-904.

4. DDT: From Cure to Curse

- Carson, R. (1962). Silent Spring. Houghton Mifflin.
- Lear, L. (1997). Rachel Carson: Witness for Nature. Henry Holt and Company.

5. Ecological Impacts of DDT

- Peakall, D. B. (1992). Animal Biomarkers as Pollution Indicators. Springer.
- Edwards, C. A. (1973). Environmental Pollution by Pesticides. Plenum Press.

6. Regulatory Changes Post-DDT

- EPA. (1975). DDT Regulatory History: A Brief Survey (to 1975). U.S. Environmental Protection Agency.

7. Integrated Pest Management (IPM)

- Kogan, M. (1998). "Integrated Pest Management: Historical Perspectives and Contemporary Developments." Annual Review of Entomology, 43, 243-270.
- Ehler, L. E. (2006). "Integrated Pest Management (IPM): Definition, Historical Development and Implementation, and the Other IPM." Pest Management Science, 62(9), 787-789.

8. Lessons from System Failures

- Perrow, C. (1999). Normal Accidents: Living with High-Risk Technologies. Princeton University Press.
- Senge, P. M. (1990). The Fifth Discipline: The Art and Practice of the Learning Organisation. Doubleday.

9. Holistic and Adaptive Planning

- Holling, C. S. (1973). "Resilience and Stability of Ecological Systems." Annual Review of Ecology and Systematics, 4, 1-23.

10. Public and Scientific Advocacy

- McCright, A. M., & Dunlap, R. E. (2011). "The Politicization of Climate Change and Polarisation in the American Public's Views of Global Warming, 2001–2010." Sociological Quarterly, 52(2), 155-194.

References and Citations for "Beyond Control" Chapter

1. Dynamic Systems and Organizational Adaptability
   - Senge, P. M. (1990). The Fifth Discipline: The Art and Practice of the Learning Organization. Doubleday.
   - Meadows, D. H. (2008). Thinking in Systems: A Primer. Chelsea Green Publishing.

2. Czar Alexander and the Challenges of Managing Complex Systems
   - Riasanovsky, N. V. (2000). A History of Russia. Oxford University Press.
   - Lieven, D. (2003). Russia Against Napoleon: The True Story of the Campaigns of War and Peace. Viking Adult.

3. Potemkin Village Effect
   - Sebag Montefiore, S. (2000). Prince of Princes: The Life of Potemkin. St. Martin's Press.

4. Volkswagen Emissions Scandal
   - Ewing, J. (2017). Faster, Higher, Farther: The Volkswagen Scandal. W. W. Norton & Company.

5. Catalytic Managership
   - Collins, J. (2001). Good to Great: Why Some Companies Make the Leap... and Others Don't. HarperCollins.

6. Flexible Systems Design
   - Brown, T., & Wyatt, J. (2010). "Design Thinking for Social Innovation." Stanford Social Innovation Review, 8(1), 30-35.
   - Ries, E. (2011). The Lean Startup: How Today's Entrepreneurs Use Continuous Innovation to Create Radically Successful Businesses. Crown Business.

7. Holacracy and Decentralized Power Structures
   - Robertson, B. J. (2015). Holacracy: The New Management System for a Rapidly Changing World. Henry Holt and Co.

8. Lessons from Nature

- Benyus, J. M. (2002). Biomimicry: Innovation Inspired by Nature. Harper Perennial.

- Holling, C. S. (1973). "Resilience and Stability of Ecological Systems." Annual Review of Ecology and Systematics, 4, 1-23.

- Kauffman, S. (1995). At Home in the Universe: The Search for the Laws of Self-Organization and Complexity. Oxford University Press.

9. Complex Systems and Organizational Behavior

- Perrow, C. (1999). Normal Accidents: Living with High-Risk Technologies. Princeton University Press.

- Weick, K. E. (1995). Sensemaking in Organizations. Sage Publications.

10. Balancing Control and Flexibility in Organizations

- Kotter, J. P. (1996). Leading Change. Harvard Business Review Press.

- Hamel, G., & Zanini, M. (2020). Humanocracy: Creating Organizations as Amazing as the People Inside Them. Harvard Business Review Press.

- Pink, D. H. (2009). Drive: The Surprising Truth About What Motivates Us. Riverhead Books.

References and Citations for "Go with the Grain" Chapter

1. Vector Theory of Systems

- Senge, P. M. (1990). The Fifth Discipline: The Art and Practice of the Learning Organization. Doubleday.

- Meadows, D. H. (2008). Thinking in Systems: A Primer. Chelsea Green Publishing.

2. The Automobile: Driving with the Human Vector

- Flink, J. J. (1988). The Automobile Age. MIT Press.

- Packer, J. (2008). Mobility Without Mayhem: Safety, Cars, and Citizenship. Duke University Press.

3. Soviet Central Planning: Swimming Against the Current

- Nove, A. (1983). The Economics of Feasible Socialism. Harper & Row.
- Conquest, R. (1990). The Great Terror: A Reassessment. Oxford University Press.

4. Finland's Educational System: Learning in Harmony

- Sahlberg, P. (2011). Finnish Lessons: What Can the World Learn from Educational Change in Finland?. Teachers College Press.
- Partanen, A. (2016). The Nordic Theory of Everything: In Search of a Better Life. HarperCollins.

5. The Toyota Production System: Flowing with Efficiency

- Liker, J. K. (2004). The Toyota Way: 14 Management Principles from the World's Greatest Manufacturer. McGraw-Hill.
- Ohno, T. (1988). Toyota Production System: Beyond Large-Scale Production. Productivity Press.

6. Southwest Airlines: Point-to-Point Precision

- Gittell, J. H. (2003). The Southwest Airlines Way: Using the Power of Relationships to Achieve High Performance. McGraw-Hill.
- Freiberg, K., & Freiberg, J. (1996). Nuts! Southwest Airlines' Crazy Recipe for Business and Personal Success. Broadway Books.

7. Buffer's Transparent Salary Formula

- Hall, E. (2016). The Culture of Technology. Counterpoint Press.
- Zappos Insights. (2010). Delivering Happiness: A Path to Profits, Passion, and Purpose. Business Plus.
- Birchfield, R. (2014). "The Transparency Movement." Management Magazine.

8. Amazon Prime: Convenience and Loyalty

- Stone, B. (2013). The Everything Store: Jeff Bezos and the Age of Amazon. Little, Brown and Company.

9. IKEA: Streamlined Simplicity

- Engwall, M. (2002). The IKEA Story. Business History Review.
- Bartlett, C. A., & Nanda, A. (1990). "Ingvar Kamprad and IKEA." Harvard Business School Case Study.

10. The U.S. Healthcare System: A Complex Maze

- Cutler, D. M. (2004). Your Money or Your Life: Strong Medicine for America's Health Care System. Oxford University Press.
- Gawande, A. (2014). Being Mortal: Medicine and What Matters in the End. Metropolitan Books.

11. Holistic Integration in System Design

- Norman, D. A. (2013). The Design of Everyday Things. Basic Books.

References and Citations for "From Design to Deviation" Chapter

1. The Cobra Effect: When Solutions Become Problems

- Siebert, H. (2001). Der Kobra-Effekt: Wie man Irrwege der Wirtschaftspolitik vermeidet. Deutsche Verlags-Anstalt.

2. Australia's Cane Toad Catastrophe

- Lever, C. (2001). The Cane Toad: The History and Ecology of a Successful Colonist. Westbury Academic and Scientific Publishing.

3. Self-Cleaning Paint vs. Graffiti Culture

- White, R. D. (2001). "Graffiti: Examining the Research Behind the Art." Crime Prevention and Community Safety, 3(2), 1-14.

4. The Unexpected Rise of E-sports

- Taylor, T. L. (2012). Raising the Stakes: E-sports and the Professionalization of Computer Gaming. MIT Press.

5. Identifying Autonomous Systems Through Early Warning Signs

- Dekker, S. (2011). Drift into Failure: From Hunting Broken Components to Understanding Complex Systems. Ashgate Publishing.
- Leveson, N. (2011). Engineering a Safer World: Systems Thinking Applied to Safety. MIT Press.

6. General System Dynamics and Feedback Mechanisms

- Forrester, J. W. (1968). Principles of Systems. Pegasus Communications.
- Meadows, D. H., Randers, J., & Meadows, D. L. (2004). The Limits to Growth: The 30-Year Update. Chelsea Green Publishing.

7. Incentive Structures and Unintended Consequences

- Gneezy, U., & Rustichini, A. (2000). "A Fine is a Price." Journal of Legal Studies, 29(1), 1-17.

- Kerr, S. (1975). "On the Folly of Rewarding A, While Hoping for B." Academy of Management Journal, 18(4), 769-783.

References and Citations for "The Perfect Error" Chapter

1. Alexander Fleming and the Discovery of Penicillin

- Fleming, A. (1929). "On the Antibacterial Action of Cultures of a Penicillium, with Special Reference to their Use in the Isolation of B. influenzae." British Journal of Experimental Pathology, 10(3), 226-236.

- Tan, S. Y., & Tatsumura, Y. (2015). "Alexander Fleming (1881-1955): Discoverer of penicillin." Singapore Medical Journal, 56(7), 366-367.

2. Post-it Notes: From Accidental Adhesion to Iconic Office Staple

- Fry, A. R. (1997). "That's the Way It Was: From Concept to Product—The Story of the Post-it Note." Journal of Chemical Education, 74(2), 241-243.

- Silver, S. (1980). "Repositionable Pressure-Sensitive Adhesive Sheet Material." US Patent 4,166,152.

3. Wilson Greatbatch and the Pacemaker

- Greatbatch, W., & Holmes, C. F. (1991). "The Implantable Cardiac Pacemaker." IEEE Transactions on Biomedical Engineering, 38(7), 645-653.

4. Dr. John O'Sullivan and the Development of Wi-Fi

- O'Sullivan, J., & Obryk, R. (1996). "The Echoes of an Exploding Black Hole: The Origins of Wi-Fi Technology." Australian Journal of Telecommunications and the Digital Economy, 4(2), 27-34.

5. Percy Spencer and the Microwave Oven

- Spencer, P. (1947). "Electromagnetic Cooking Device." US Patent 2,495,429.

- Whiteside, T. (1972). The Microwave Oven: A Milestone in Culinary Convenience. Doubleday.

6. Dr. Harry Coover and Super Glue
   - Coover, H. (1958). "Alkyl 2-Cyanoacrylates." US Patent 2,768,109.
   - "The Accidental Adhesive: The Story of Super Glue." (2008). Popular Mechanics, 185(2), 56-59.

7. Wilhelm Conrad Röntgen and the Discovery of X-rays
   - Röntgen, W. C. (1895). "On a New Kind of Rays." Nature, 53, 274-276.
   - Glasser, O. (1933). Wilhelm Conrad Röntgen and the Early History of the X-ray. C. C. Thomas Publisher.

8. George de Mestral and the Invention of Velcro
   - De Mestral, G. (1955). "Hook and Loop Fastening Device." US Patent 2,717,437.
   - "Velcro: Nature's Blueprint for Innovation." (2009). Scientific American, 300(4), 32-37.

9. Andre Geim, Konstantin Novoselov, and the Discovery of Graphene
   - Geim, A. K., & Novoselov, K. S. (2007). "The Rise of Graphene." Nature Materials, 6(3), 183-191.
   - "Nobel Prize in Physics 2010: Graphene—Materials of the Future." (2010). Nobel Prize Official Document.

10. Viagra: From Heart Medicine to Erection Pill
    - "Viagra's Journey: From Heart Med to Game-Changer in ED Treatment." (2000). The Lancet, 355(9199), 1787-1788.

11. Lithium-ion Batteries
    - Yoshino, A. (1987). "Secondary Battery Comprising Lithium-Doped Cathode." US Patent 4,668,595.
    - "Nobel Prize in Chemistry 2019: The Development of Lithium-ion Batteries." (2019). Nobel Prize Official Document.

12. General Theories on Embracing Errors in System Design
    - Tenner, E. (1997). Why Things Bite Back: Technology and the Revenge of Unintended Consequences. Vintage Books.

References and Citations for "The Metric Mishap" Chapter

1. Mars Climate Orbiter Incident

   - "Mars Climate Orbiter Mishap Investigation Board Report." NASA, November 1999.

2. Organisational Collaboration and Communication

   - Pinto, J. K., & Slevin, D. P. (1988). "Critical Success Factors in Effective Project Implementation." IEEE Transactions on Engineering Management, 34(1), 22-27.

3. Home Depot's Expansion into China

   - "The Failure of Home Depot in China." (2012). Harvard Business Review.

   - Yang, X., & Yu, S. (2012). "Why Home Depot Failed in China." Forbes.

4. Starbucks in Australia

   - "Starbucks: Failure in Australia." (2008). Case Study. INSEAD.

   - "Starbucks' Australian Demise: Analyzing the Missteps." (2014). Journal of Business Strategy, 35(1), 35-40.

5. Principles for Fault-Tolerant Systems

   - Perrow, C. (1984). Normal Accidents: Living with High-Risk Technologies. Basic Books.

   - Dekker, S. (2006). The Field Guide to Understanding Human Error. Ashgate Publishing.

6. Precision in Systems Operations

   - "Precision in Engineering and its Importance in Industry." (2018). Engineering Management Journal, 30(3), 145-152.

7. Harmonisation of Standards

   - "Global Standards and Their Role in Promoting Interoperability." (2016). Journal of Global Information Management, 24(1), 19-37.

8. Integrated Systems Thinking

   - Senge, P. M. (1990). The Fifth Discipline: The Art & Practice of The Learning Organization. Doubleday.

   - Checkland, P., & Scholes, J. (1990). Soft Systems Methodology in Action. Wiley.

9. Risk Management through Redundancy

- Reason, J. (1997). Managing the Risks of Organizational Accidents. Ashgate Publishing.
- Leveson, N. G. (2011). Engineering a Safer World: Systems Thinking Applied to Safety. MIT Press.

References and Citations for "Growth Unchecked" Chapter

1. Cyril Northcote Parkinson and Parkinson's Law

- Parkinson, C. N. (1958). Parkinson's Law: The Pursuit of Progress. John Murray.

2. Big-Bang Theorem of Systems-Cosmology

- Arthur, W. B. (1994). Increasing Returns and Path Dependence in the Economy. University of Michigan Press.

3. Roman Empire: Over-expansion and Its Pitfalls

- Heather, P. (2006). The Fall of the Roman Empire: A New History of Rome and the Barbarians. Oxford University Press.
- Goldsworthy, A. (2009). How Rome Fell: Death of a Superpower. Yale University Press.

4. Amazon Web Services (AWS)

- Iyer, B., & Henderson, J. C. (2010). "Preparing for the Future: Understanding the Seven Capabilities of Cloud Computing." MIS Quarterly Executive, 9(2), 117-131.

5. Internal and External Forces in System Growth

- Senge, P. M. (1990). The Fifth Discipline: The Art and Practice of the Learning Organization. Doubleday.
- Kotter, J. P. (1996). Leading Change. Harvard Business Review Press.

6. Efficiency Loss and Vulnerability Increase

- Tushman, M. L., & O'Reilly, C. A. (1997). Winning Through Innovation: A Practical Guide to Leading Organizational Change and Renewal. Harvard Business Review Press.

7. Mastering the Growth Game

- Hamel, G., & Prahalad, C. K. (1994). Competing for the Future. Harvard Business Review Press.

8. The Complexity Paradox and Law of Diminishing Returns
   - Simon, H.A. (1962). "The Architecture of Complexity." Proceedings of the American Philosophical Society, 106(6), 467-482.
   - Mankiw, N. G. (2014). Principles of Economics. Cengage Learning.

9. Entropy in Organisations
   - Hannan, M. T., & Freeman, J. (1989). Organizational Ecology. Harvard University Press.
   - Ashkenas, R., Ulrich, D., Jick, T., & Kerr, S. (2002). The Boundaryless Organization: Breaking the Chains of Organizational Structure. Jossey-Bass.

10. Ecosystem Analogy and Strategic Saturation
   - Levin, S. A. (1998). "Ecosystems and the Biosphere as Complex Adaptive Systems." Ecosystems, 1(5), 431-436.
   - Drucker, P. F. (2001). The Essential Drucker: The Best of Sixty Years of Peter Drucker's Essential Writings on Management. HarperCollins.

References and Citations for "Systemic Resistance" Chapter

1. Le Chatelier's Principle and Systemic Resistance
   - Le Chatelier, H. L. (1884). «Sur un énoncé général des lois des équilibres chimiques.» Comptes rendus de l'Académie des Sciences, 99, 786-789.

2. Misaligned Feedback Mechanisms
   - Argyris, C. (1999). On Organizational Learning. Blackwell Publishers.
   - Forrester, J. W. (1961). Industrial Dynamics. MIT Press.

3. Systemic Inertia and the Perpetual Loop
   - Hannan, M. T., & Freeman, J. (1989). Organizational Ecology. Harvard University Press.

4. The Resilience Paradox and Bureaucratic Entropy
   - Ashkenas, R., Ulrich, D., Jick, T., & Kerr, S. (2002). The Boundaryless Organization: Breaking the Chains of Organizational Structure. Jossey-Bass.

5. Cultural Inertia
   - Cameron, K. S., & Quinn, R. E. (2011). Diagnosing and Changing Organizational Culture: Based on the Competing Values Framework. Jossey-Bass.
   - Schein, E. H. (2010). Organizational Culture and Leadership. Jossey-Bass.

6. Feedback Fidelity
   - Wiener, N. (1948). Cybernetics: Or Control and Communication in the Animal and the Machine. MIT Press.
   - Sterman, J. D. (2000). Business Dynamics: Systems Thinking and Modeling for a Complex World. McGraw-Hill Education.

7. Systemic Adaptation vs. Adoption
   - Christensen, C. M., & Overdorf, M. (2000). "Meeting the Challenge of Disruptive Change." Harvard Business Review, 78(2), 66-76.
   - Rogers, E. M. (2003). Diffusion of Innovations. Free Press.

8. Simplicity in Complexity
   - Maeda, J. (2006). The Laws of Simplicity. MIT Press.
   - Norman, D. A. (2013). The Design of Everyday Things. Basic Books.

References and Citations for "Slack in System Design" Chapter

1. Introduction to System Design and Efficiency
   - Hollnagel, E. (2006). Resilience Engineering: Concepts and Precepts. Ashgate Publishing.

2. Modern Electrical Grids and Vulnerability
   - U.S.-Canada Power System Outage Task Force (2004). Final Report on the August 14, 2003 Blackout in the United States and Canada: Causes and Recommendations. U.S. Department of Energy and Natural Resources Canada.

3. Financial Systems and the 2008 Financial Crisis
   - Brunnermeier, M. K. (2009). "Deciphering the Liquidity and Credit Crunch 2007-2008." Journal of Economic Perspectives, 23(1), 77-100.

4. Tokyo's Rail System
   - Okumura, E., & Takahashi, T. (2009). "Tokyo's Rail Network: Real-Time Congestion Prediction and Measures." International Journal of Intelligent Transportation Systems Research, 7, 53-61.

5. The Elastic Principle and Internet Infrastructure
   - Cerf, V. G. (2019). A Brief History of the Internet. ACM SIGCOMM Computer Communication Review.

6. The Diversity Buffer in Nature
   - Tilman, D. (1999). "The Ecological Consequences of Changes in Biodiversity: A Search for General Principles." Ecology, 80(5), 1455-1474.

7. Redundancy in Systems
   - Laprie, J. C., et al. (1992). Dependability: Basic Concepts and Terminology. Springer-Verlag.

8. Adaptation Over Optimisation
   - Holland, J. H. (1992). Adaptation in Natural and Artificial Systems. MIT Press.

9. Deep Insights
   - Peters, T. J., & Waterman, R. H. (1982). In Search of Excellence: Lessons from America's Best-Run Companies. Harper & Row.

References and Citations for "Fail-Safe Design" Chapter

1. Introduction to Fail-Safe Systems
   - Perrow, C. (1999). Normal Accidents: Living with High-Risk Technologies. Princeton University Press.

2. Historical Failures and Lessons Learned
   - Medvedev, G. (1991). The Truth About Chernobyl. Basic Books.

3. Contemporary Challenges in Fail-Safe Design
   - Funabashi, Y., & Kitazawa, K. (2012). "Fukushima in review: A complex disaster, a disastrous response." Bulletin of the Atomic Scientists, 68(2), 9-21.

4. Evolving Fail-Safe Technologies

- Goodall, N. J. (2014). "Machine Ethics and Automated Vehicles." In Road Vehicle Automation (pp. 93-102). Springer, Cham.

5. Deep Insights

- Taleb, N. N. (2012). Antifragile: Things That Gain from Disorder. Random House.

- Leveson, N. G. (2012). Engineering a Safer World: Systems Thinking Applied to Safety. MIT Press.

References and Citations for "Symphony of Complexity" Chapter

1. Understanding Complexity and the Kantian Hypothesis

- Kant, I. (1998). Critique of Pure Reason. Cambridge University Press. (Original work published 1781).

2. Principle 1: Mastery of Simplicity

- Maeda, J. (2006). The Laws of Simplicity. MIT Press.

3. Principle 2: Architecting Redundancy

- Perrow, C. (1999). Normal Accidents: Living with High-Risk Technologies. Princeton University Press.

4. Principle 3: Decentralisation Dynamo

- Barabási, A. L. (2003). Linked: How Everything Is Connected to Everything Else and What It Means for Business, Science, and Everyday Life. Plume.

5. Principle 4: Emergent Symphony

- Holland, J. H. (1998). Emergence: From Chaos to Order. Basic Books.

6. Principle 5: Chaos Harmony

- Gleick, J. (1987). Chaos: Making a New Science. Viking.

7. Principle 6: Evolutionary Pulse

- Darwin, C. (1859). On the Origin of Species by Means of Natural Selection. John Murray.

8. Principle 7: Feedback Fusion

- Sterman, J. D. (2000). Business Dynamics: Systems Thinking and Modeling for a Complex World. McGraw-Hill Education.

9. Principle 8: Human-Centric Harmony

- Norman, D. A. (2013). The Design of Everyday Things: Revised and Expanded Edition. Basic Books.

10. Principle 9: Cross-Disciplinary Fusion

- Thagard, P. (2012). The Cognitive Science of Science: Explanation, Discovery, and Conceptual Change. MIT Press.

11. Principle 10: Simplicity Zen

- Maeda, J. (2006). The Laws of Simplicity. MIT Press.

References and Citations for "The Power of Starting Simple" Chapter

1. Simplicity in Design and the principles

- Maeda, J. (2006). The Laws of Simplicity. MIT Press.
- The Strategy of Reduction
- Tharp, T., & Reiter, M. (2003). The Creative Habit: Learn It and Use It for Life. Simon & Schuster.

2. Measuring Simplicity

- Tullis, T., & Albert, B. (2013). Measuring the User Experience: Collecting, Analyzing, and Presenting Usability Metrics. Morgan Kaufmann.

3. Affordance Theory

- Norman, D. A. (1988). The Psychology of Everyday Things. Basic Books.

4. Cognitive Load Theory

- Sweller, J. (1988). "Cognitive load during problem solving: Effects on learning." Cognitive Science, 12(2), 257-285.

5. Principles of Behaviour Design

- Fogg, B. J. (2009). Fogg Behavior Model. Behavior Model Website.

6. Psychology of Simplicity

- Schwartz, B. (2004). The Paradox of Choice: Why More Is Less. HarperCollins.
- Kahneman, D. (2011). Thinking, Fast and Slow. Farrar, Straus and Giroux.

7. Human-Centric Harmony and Cross-Disciplinary Fusion

- Norman, D. A. (2013). The Design of Everyday Things: Revised and Expanded Edition. Basic Books.

References and Citations for "Aboriginal Wisdom: Building Systems That Last" Chapter

1. The Ingenious Fish Traps of Brewarrina (Ngunnhu)

- Morphy, H., & Smith, B. (Eds.). (1991). The Art of Bark Painting: Reflections on the Enduring Tradition of Aboriginal Art. Cambridge University Press..

2. Aboriginal Water Management Systems

- McNiven, I. J., & Russell, L. (2005). Appropriated Pasts: Indigenous Peoples and the Colonial Culture of Archaeology. AltaMira Press.

3. Aboriginal Fire Management Systems

- Gammage, B. (2011). The Biggest Estate on Earth: How Aborigines Made Australia. Allen & Unwin.
- Bowman, D. M., et al. (2009). "Fire Regimes and the Cultural Landscapes of Indigenous Australians." Proceedings of the Royal Society B: Biological Sciences, 276(1667), 479-487.

4. Aboriginal Trade Systems

- Mulvaney, D. J., & Kamminga, J. (1999). Prehistory of Australia. Smithsonian Institution Press.
- Clarke, P. (2003). Where the Ancestors Walked: Australia as an Aboriginal Landscape. Allen & Unwin.

5. Aboriginal Knowledge Systems

- Reynolds, H. (1981). The Other Side of the Frontier: Aboriginal Resistance to the European Invasion of Australia. Penguin Books.
- Sutton, P. (1998). Dreamings: The Art of Aboriginal Australia. Viking.

6. Coolamons: Ergonomic and Versatile Design

- Berndt, R. M., & Berndt, C. H. (1992). The World of the First Australians. Aboriginal Studies Press.

- Tindale, N. B. (1974). Aboriginal Tribes of Australia: Their Terrain, Environmental Controls, Distribution, Limits, and Proper Names. Australian National University Press.

7. Woomera: Enhancing Human Capability

- Davidson, D. S. (1936). Aboriginal Australian and Tasmanian Weapons. American Anthropologist, 38(4), 538-564.

- Akerman, K., & Bindon, P. (1995). "Woomera: The Aboriginal Spear Thrower in the West." Australian Aboriginal Studies, 1995(2), 68-72.

8. Building a Future with Enduring Systems

- Diamond, J. (2005). Collapse: How Societies Choose to Fail or Succeed. Viking Press.

- Meadows, D. H., Randers, J., & Meadows, D. L. (2004). Limits to Growth: The 30-Year Update. Chelsea Green Publishing.

www.ingramcontent.com/pod-product-compliance
Lightning Source LLC
Chambersburg PA
CBHW041256040426
42334CB00028BA/3043